The Ultimate Guide to Implementing Wellbeing Programmes for School

This is an essential guide for all teaching professionals to help them make an informed decision about what wellbeing programmes and initiatives they should select in their schools and why. It provides teachers and school leaders with all necessary knowledge to help identify what they should be looking for in wellbeing programmes, how they should be evaluating its effectiveness and who should be delivering it for them. It presents a suite of components and evidence-based interventions that teachers can pick and choose for their school community.

For the first time, practitioners are not being sold a specific programme but presented instead with what is known about wellbeing in order to empower them to make their own decisions that best suit their community. It goes behind the scenes and reveals the secrets used by researchers and experts, including practical advice, recommendations and the author's own ground-breaking research study involving 3,000 students. Its unique pick-and-mix process demystifies programme creation, simplifies it and makes its building blocks available to the masses.

This accessible, evidence-based guide suggests a whole-school approach with specific interventions that can be used to successfully improve the wellbeing of teachers and students, making it an invaluable resource and must-read for all teaching professionals.

Jolanta Burke, Ph.D., chartered educational psychologist with the British Psychological Society, is an assistant professor and researcher in Maynooth University, where she teaches wellbeing for Master's in Education and Master's in Educational Leadership and Management. For her work on wellbeing, she was acknowledged by the Irish Times as one of 30 people in Ireland who make it a better place. For more information, visit www.jolantaburke.com.

If you care about the wellbeing of your students, you must read this book. Through the theory and practice of wellbeing in schools, Dr Burke is taking us on a fascinating journey of a child's and school community's wellbeing. It is all you need to know to create a wellbeing strategy in schools. The book is fresh, balanced, and highly recommended.

Dr Itai Ivtzan, Positive Psychologist and Associate Professor, Naropa University, Boulder, USA

This book is based firmly in positive psychology research and gives a solid rationale for why wellbeing is so central for all students. It is a volume of considerable depth and does not duck the challenges of context, the complexity of the concept, the resistance of some educators to fitting in yet another initiative, nor the problems associated with seeking 'happiness'. Importantly it places teacher wellbeing at the heart of a whole-school approach and the centrality of caring school leadership for effective change. The theory is enhanced with the author's own experiences, reflections and stories of practice from around the world. This is a welcome text for educators who want something more substantial than a simple 'why what and how' of wellbeing.

Dr Sue Roffey, Ted-X speaker, Founder of the Wellbeing Australia Network

Wellbeing in schools has rightly become an important and even urgent topic. But it is a complex issue and needs to be understood and approached in a careful and evidenced-based way. In that respect, this book is a wonderful guide to the latest research and theories in this area, together with practical ideas and resources for how to actually implement these insights. Very clear and easy to read, this is an indispensable book for anyone interested in how to help children and young people flourish at school and in their lives as a whole.

Dr Tim Lomas, Senior Lecturer in Applied Positive Psychology, University of East London, UK

The Ultimate Guide to Implementing Wellbeing Programmes for School

Jolanta Burke

LONDON AND NEW YORK

First published 2021
by Routledge
2 Park Square, Milton Park, Abingdon, Oxon OX14 4RN

and by Routledge
52 Vanderbilt Avenue, New York, NY 10017

Routledge is an imprint of the Taylor & Francis Group, an informa business

© 2021 Jolanta Burke

The right of Jolanta Burke to be identified as author of this work has been asserted by her in accordance with sections 77 and 78 of the Copyright, Designs and Patents Act 1988.

All rights reserved. No part of this book may be reprinted or reproduced or utilised in any form or by any electronic, mechanical or other means, now known or hereafter invented, including photocopying and recording, or in any information storage or retrieval system, without permission in writing from the publishers.

Trademark notice: Product or corporate names may be trademarks or registered trademarks, and are used only for identification and explanation without intent to infringe.

British Library Cataloguing-in-Publication Data
A catalogue record for this book is available from the British Library

Library of Congress Cataloging-in-Publication Data
Names: Burke, Jolanta, author.
Title: The ultimate guide to implementing wellbeing programmes for school / Jolanta Burke.
Identifiers: LCCN 2020038763 | ISBN 9780367902261 (hardback) | ISBN 9780367902278 (paperback) | ISBN 9781003023258 (ebook)
Subjects: LCSH: School mental health services. | Teachers--Mental health services.
Classification: LCC LB3430 .B87 2021 | DDC 371.7/13--dc23
LC record available at https://lccn.loc.gov/2020038763

ISBN: 978-0-367-90226-1 (hbk)
ISBN: 978-0-367-90227-8 (pbk)
ISBN: 978-1-003-02325-8 (ebk)

Typeset in Bembo
by SPi Global, India

Contents

Acknowledgement vii
About the author ix
Preface xi

1 Introduction 1

2 Making sense of the complex world of wellbeing 18

3 Your guide to the essential elements of wellbeing 29

4 The mechanisms that enable successful wellbeing interventions 77

5 A review of established school wellbeing programmes 96

6 Your guide to making the best-informed decisions 102

Author index 109
Subject index 111

Acknowledgements

This book is dedicated to Jack, who has made me 'beyond' happy, a place I never thought existed, until the day he was born.

I would like to thank Bren, mum, Charlie, auntie Ira and the rest of my family for their ongoing love and support. I wish to thank all my friends, Iwona, Anne, Deirdre, Seamus, Julie, Sandy, Martin and JP for their friendship, constant support and bearing with me through all the years of ups and downs. I feel so lucky to live and grow amid a bunch of such wonderful people.

I also wish to thank my colleagues at Maynooth University, who have inspired me with our discussions and chats every day, Dr Majella Dempsey, Dr Olive Laffoy, Dr Catriona O'Toole, Dr Grace O'Grady, Dr Celine Healy, Prof. Aislinn O'Donnell, Prof. Sharon Todd, Paula Kinnarney, Dr Maija Salokangas, Brenda O'Carroll, Fiona Casey, Brona O'Brien, Georgina Sherlock, Grace Holmes, Dr Anthony Malone, Dr Joe Oyler, Dr Tom Walsh, Angela Rickard, Dr Zerrin Doganca Kucuc and many others. Thank you all for your wise words and support. I really appreciate it.

About the author

Jolanta Burke, Ph.D., is a chartered educational psychologist (British Psychological Society), assistant professor and researcher in Maynooth University, where she teaches wellbeing for Master's in Education and Master's in Educational Leadership and Management. She completed her Ph.D. at Trinity College Dublin, in the field of Positive Education.

Before joining Maynooth University, she was a programme leader and a senior lecturer for Master's in Applied Positive Psychology and Coaching Psychology at the University of East London, which is the hub of the European research in wellbeing. Prior to this, she lectured in Dublin City University and Trinity Business School where she designed and delivered a highly popular module in Psychology of Leadership for a Master's in Management programme, subsequently awarded the top general management master's degree in Western Europe, and the Trinity MBA programme.

She has spoken at conferences around the world and published extensively. She is an editor-in-chief of the peer-reviewed Journal in Positive School Psychology. For her work on wellbeing, she was acknowledged by the Irish Times as one of 30 people in Ireland who make it a better place. For more information, please go to www.jolantaburke.com.

Preface

Purpose of the book

The aim of this book is to help you design an evidence-informed wellbeing strategy for your school. It was written with a practitioner in mind to assist you in making a positive difference to your pre-school, primary- and secondary-school community. It is written for school leaders who are responsible for implementing the wellbeing initiatives in schools, teachers whose remit is an introduction of wellbeing initiatives in their school, as well as all other teachers, for whom their school's community wellbeing is important. It is also written for community health and wellbeing coordinators who want to enhance their educational community's wellbeing. Regardless of who you are, I do hope you will find it useful.

Over the years, I have received frequent emails from school professionals and educational organisations with requests to enlighten them about wellbeing in schools. They have been asking me why wellbeing became such a critical focus for the ministry/department of education in their countries, they enquired into what research says about wellbeing, what programmes to choose, and finally, if I could recommend a book that helps them make a decision. In response, I have usually sent them a long email about it but always found it difficult to recommend a book that would clarify some of their queries. Most books promote their own programmes and wellbeing frameworks, rather than review what is out there that can be used. I have no frameworks, interventions or programmes to promote. The book is, therefore, written with honesty and as much objectivity as I could fashion. Being a psychologist specialising in positive psychology, my views are slightly biased towards the field, but I tried hard to be balanced in my approach and incorporate non-positive-psychological perspectives too. Please note that throughout the book, I usually refer to children as students, regardless of their age. While the book was written primarily with students in mind, it can be, and should be used within the entire school community.

When writing it, I wanted to make sure that all the advice I offer you is evidence based; therefore, the entire book is peppered with references of the research I drew from. If you are interested in exploring it further, please feel free to look up the academic papers and books I have quoted. Also, at the end of the book, you will find some interesting additional resources you can use to deepen your knowledge about this topic.

How to read it?

I recommend that you read the book in the order it is written, as each chapter builds on the previous chapter's knowledge. Once you have read it, you can go back and forth to various parts that provide you with some practical tools on how to implement wellbeing strategy for your school. Throughout the book, you will find plenty of interventions that have been tested within various international communities. I suggest you familiarise yourselves with them and work with your team on tweaking them so that they best suit your specific community. This is why, unless it is a borrowed book, I encourage you to take plenty of notes in the book margin or in your e-book. This will help you assimilate the new research more effectively and help you apply it in your school. Also, please highlight the sections that you might want to quickly go back to when you are creating your own school's wellbeing strategy. I have mixed the theory with practice throughout, so these sections are important to note, especially if they are applicable to you.

Make this book your own and choose to take whatever ideas you wish from it. For some of you, the book will serve as a step-by-step guide to the process on how to strategise for wellbeing in school. For others, it will help you understand the bigger picture of all you need to know about the evidence behind wellbeing and its application in schools. As long as you take a few ideas from it and introduce them in your school, I hope it will make a positive difference to your community. The book is entitled an "Ultimate guide…" because it provides you with the foundations for designing an evidence-informed wellbeing strategy in your school.

Structure of the book

The book is divided into six chapters.

The first chapter will introduce you to some of the challenges that exist in relation to creating a wellbeing strategy in schools, such as the current perception of wellbeing. We will then look at how the school environment affects students' wellbeing. Even though it is not the primary focus of the book, it is a critical part of a well-designed strategy for wellbeing, therefore needs to be considered, before we delve deeper into interventions and programmes we can create for the school community members.

The second chapter will help you make sense of the complex world of wellbeing. We will look at some definitions of wellbeing and try to define a complex notion that has grown exponentially in many different directions. I will then give you a whistle-stop-tour of the main concepts and some significant findings that can inform your school's wellbeing strategy. This chapter will also provide you with some of the most common frameworks and models of wellbeing, which you can apply in your school. The objective of this chapter is to explain all the main research findings relating to wellbeing and provide you with a bigger picture of what it is all about.

The third chapter is somewhat a continuation of the second one. The finishing argument in the previous chapter is that the current models of wellbeing are componential, meaning that they consist of a number of components that researchers deem important. In this chapter, I will briefly introduce you to the main components of the wellbeing models and offer you some interventions relating to them so that you can use the evidence-based intervention and adapt them to your school community. Apart from the existing components, I will also present a number of additional components that are school related and which I suggest you may consider when creating your school's wellbeing strategy. The objective of this chapter is to provide you with pick-and-mix components that may serve as a part of a framework for wellbeing in your school.

The fourth chapter will review some of the research-based mechanisms that enable the wellbeing interventions and programmes to work. By understanding why and how the activities work, you will be able to create an optimal wellbeing strategy that will keep your students become fully engaged throughout. Most importantly, however, knowing the mechanisms of wellbeing interventions will provide you with the confidence to experiment with the dosage, variety and other components of wellbeing interventions. The objective of this chapter is to provide you with a list of mechanisms to evaluate the effectiveness of the wellbeing programmes and interventions in school.

The fifth chapter will review some of the evaluated programmes available for students at different levels and their components. I will introduce you to an evaluation process that will assist you in analysing the effectiveness and appropriateness of any wellbeing programme that comes your way and is available in your geographical proximity. This knowledge will allow you to make informed-decisions as to whether or not the programme is applicable to your school and will serve your school community well. The objective of this chapter is to equip you with wellbeing programme evaluation skills.

The sixth chapter will provide you with a step-by-step guide for creating your school's optimal wellbeing strategy. Drawing from past research on the effectiveness of such initiatives, it will provide you with simple guidelines of not only what to do but also how to do it. The objective of this chapter is to help you design and deliver a successful wellbeing strategy for your school.

I look forward to taking you on a journey of wellbeing, a topic I am very passionate about and which I hope you already do, and will share with me by the end of reading this book. I would like to learn your thoughts about the book or your reflections about the application of the advice from the book in your school. Please go to www.jolantaburke.com to contact me.

CHAPTER

Introduction

I recently attended a talk organised for educators from primary and post-primary schools, during which a speaker asked the audience to guestimate the extent to which our youth experience mental health issues. It was astounding how much the group has underestimated the statistics.

Worldwide, between 10 and 20% of young people experience diagnosed mental health issues (WHO, 2019). The operative word here is "diagnosed" because the number of undiagnosed cases are estimated to be at least double this (Oliver et al., 2008). The worrying fact is that increasingly more children as young as 2 years are diagnosed with mental health problems (Costello et al., 2003). One in eight 5–19 year olds has reported at least one mental health disorder, and their prevalence continues to rise year-on-year (GOV.UK, 2018). Suicide is now the third leading cause of death in 15–19 year olds and the second cause of death in adolescent girls (WHO, 2018a). Girls score lower than boys across most of the wellbeing indicators, and the wellbeing of both genders decreases steadily, as they move towards adulthood (Burke and Minton, 2019). The COVID pandemic further exasperated young people's wellbeing, aspects of which had reduced compared to pre-crisis levels (Quinn et al., 2020). These staggering statistics continue to shock, as we see a growing number of young people engaging in self-harm, experiencing obesity, abusing alcohol, drugs, smoking and embarking on early sexual initiation.

It is no wonder that international organisations are frantically introducing wellbeing programmes and strategies to try to reduce these numbers. The World Health Organisation (WHO) has created a comprehensive mental health action plan for 2013–2020 (Shrivastava et al., 2015). UNESCO has introduced a strategy on education for health and wellbeing (UNESCO, 2016), UNICEF has promoted its strategy for health (2016–2030) (UNICEF, 2016) and in 2013 the United Nations launched International Happiness Day as a preamble to their 17 Sustainable Development Goals which seek to enhance wellbeing and happiness (UN, 2020). These are just some of the international organisations that put mental health first.

Globally, country governments followed suit introducing their own versions of wellbeing strategies and promoting measures of personal wellbeing at a national level.

One of the first ones was the government of Bhutan that made happiness their priority by incorporating it into their constitution and deeming it more important than the pursuit of Gross National Product (Harford, 2019). In 2010, the UK government launched their wellbeing policy (GOV.UK, 2013) along with other European countries, such as France, Germany, the Netherlands, Italy, Spain (Kroll and Delhey, 2013). In 2019, New Zealand announced the creation of the first "wellbeing budget" in the world (Bloomfield, 2019). By 2020, The government of the Republic of Ireland announced that by 2020 all secondary schools would be required to introduce at least 400 timetabled hours of wellbeing for young people aged 12–14 years old (EDUCATION.IE, 2019). While not much guidance has been initially given to schools as to how they are supposed to do it, it resulted in schools becoming creative with the types of programmes and interventions they introduce.

There is a wide spectrum of health-related and/or wellbeing programmes and interventions delivered in schools. Programmes refer to structured series of events designed to increase aspects of wellbeing, for example, *Zippy Friends* enhancing coping skills (Bale and Mishara, 2004). Interventions are intentional activities designed to boost an element of wellbeing, which can be introduced as part of a class, programme or schoolwide, for example, *Loving Kindness Meditation* (Fredrickson et al., 2008), or performing *Not-so-random Acts of Kindness* (Binfet, 2015). In addition to wellbeing programmes and interventions, in this book I urge you to consider creating a comprehensive strategy for wellbeing. A strategy that would incorporate planned, long-term (2–3 years), medium-term (1 year) and short-term (the next few weeks and months) activities, all of which would be aligned with the school needs and a specific wellbeing framework. This systematic approach to wellbeing delivery will set your school up for success (Murphy and Baines, 2015) and prevent you from introducing ad hoc bursts of initiatives that tick off the box for implanting *some* wellbeing in schools, but may have very little effect on students' wellness.

Issues with wellbeing

Even though wellbeing is like a velcro, sticking to all school-related activities and has become an integral part of our lives, we tend to have an equivocal relationship with it. On the one hand, we all understand how important it is for our school community; on the other hand, we recognise there are many issues associated with wellbeing provision in educational settings. Here are just a few examples of these issues.

Wicked wellbeing

The more the governments and international organisations push schools to deliver wellbeing and put it high up on the school agenda, the more frustrating it becomes for some teachers and school leaders to do it. This is why some educational researchers began to provocatively refer to it as "health fascism" (Fitzpatrick and Tinning, 2014) or a "wicked problem" (Bache et al., 2016). Recently, I have also heard several teachers alluding to it being a "dirty" word, because each time someone in the staff-room mentions wellbeing, teachers' stress levels rise. They all know how important wellbeing is for their students, they know how highly the Department of Education rates it, they also know that they are meant to introduce it in their classes, but many of them are confused as to what exactly is expected of them or what this elusive wellbeing is all about. This lack of clarity and associated mixed-emotions create negative connotations with wellbeing, making it a "dirty" word.

One reason for these mixed-emotions is that, after all, teachers are not mental health professionals, counsellors or therapists, yet they are often required to act as such. It makes many of them uncomfortable and, frankly, it could be dangerous for the children too. In many professions, such as coaching, we train professionals to recognise their own limitations and give clear guidelines as to when they should refer their clients to a therapist (Burke, 2018). Yet, in some schools, teachers are not only required to deal with tricky situations, for which they have not been trained, but they may also be asked to deliver wellbeing interventions, of which they know very little. They may teach biology, mathematics or languages expertly, but they certainly do not consider themselves experts in wellbeing. Expectations of teachers that are unrealistic, or unreasonable, such as wellbeing-related expectations, result in the reduction of teachers' wellbeing and their effectiveness (Wigford and Higgins, 2019). This is why care needs to be taken when implementing wellbeing programmes and interventions to make sure teachers are clear as to the limits of their required work.

A group of my Masters-in-Education students (Miriam Fitzgerald, Kellie Keenan, and Gemma McGill) have recently carried out a series of in-depth interviews with teachers tasked to teach students wellbeing in secondary schools in Ireland. What they found was that, firstly, wellbeing teachers felt that their subject was undervalued by other teachers, which made them shy away from telling the world about wellbeing and made them even less likely to help their colleagues improve their wellbeing when they struggled. Secondly, their knowledge of the subject was ad hoc, as despite teaching wellbeing, they didn't have any clarity as to what it was about. So much so, that they even found it difficult to define it and were unable to discuss the frameworks they used in relation to their taught subject. Stuck between the negative perception of wellbeing, and not quite knowing what they can do to enhance students' wellbeing, their own experience of the subject has become largely negative, making wellbeing a slippery slope for the wellbeing teachers and schools.

Harmful wellbeing

Pressured to do something they don't know much about, because they were not formally trained to attend to it, teachers resort to designing programmes and interventions by picking up ideas from Ted-talks, reading pop-psychology books, or chatting with their friends and colleagues from other schools who recommend specific programmes that worked for them. However, this approach is like asking Dr Google what is wrong with us when we have a headache. Based on the results, we might come up with some incorrect conclusions, simply because we are unable to see the bigger picture. The same applies to wellbeing. Introducing wellbeing initiatives in school without the knowledge of the bigger picture of wellbeing can be not only ineffective but also harmful. Here are a few examples of how we could get wellbeing wrong.

Expressing gratitude is a simple activity often recommended by some popular psychology books (Brown, 2012; Lyubomirsky, 2007). Many interventions have been developed, the objective of which was to become more grateful about our lives and see the good things that our lives are made of (Emmons and McCullough, 2003). Indeed, research suggests that changing our perspective to more grateful may prove useful for us. It strengthens bonds between people, improving their relationships for up to 6 months (Algoe et al., 2013), it enhances our capacity to forgive (DeShea, 2003), and it helps us cope more effectively with stressful situations, making it easier for students to deal with adversity (Fredrickson et al., 2003). All this research often makes people want to practice it daily and, indeed, some pop-psychology writers encourage others to do so. However, research is also showing us that the activity is less effective when practiced too frequently (Lyubomirsky et al., 2005), simply because we get bored with it and it becomes a chore for us, rather than a source of enhanced wellbeing.

Another example of a possibly negative effect of a wellbeing intervention is the whole concept of positive affirmations. Introduced and publicised heavily by Louise Hay (1984), it encouraged us to keep repeating in our heads positive thoughts about self, in the times of despair, or uncertainty, such as "I am a lovable person." When I worked with people with depression, they used to tell me how much they hated when someone encouraged them to do self-affirmations, as sometimes they made them feel more desperate. While there are advantages to some people in practicing positive affirmations (Howell, 2017), research supports their views showing that this activity is not effective for people with lower self-esteem, as it makes them feel worse about themselves (Wood et al., 2009). Therefore, care needs to be taken when using pop-psychology interventions to enhance students' wellbeing in school, as some approaches may be harmful.

Elusive wellbeing

Another problem we are facing in relation to wellbeing is the elusive nature of it. There is a confusion about what constitutes wellbeing. From the medical perspective, it is referred to as mental health, and from the philosophical and psychological perspective, it is called wellbeing (Svane et al., 2019) and yet there are other terms that describe is as happiness, wellness or welfare to mention but a few. Even the spelling of the word *wellbeing* is confusing, as we call it wellbeing, well-being, or well being.

In addition to this, the conceptualisation of wellbeing is also different. For instance, rates of mental illness double after natural disasters and war inception (WHO, 2014) which is why for individuals and societies experiencing war and political upheaval, wellbeing is about moving from violence to peace. Similarly, according to a Lancet study (Richter et al., 2017), 43% of children below 5 years old from low- and middle-income countries are at risk of poor health and nutrition. Therefore, for people living in underdeveloped countries, where poverty is widespread, wellbeing is about moving from the misery of poverty to having enough sustenance to sustain existence. However, the most salient approach to wellbeing in school is a medical or psychological perspective, and to lesser degree a philosophical view, which are described in this text.

Health refers to "a state of complete physical, mental and social wellbeing" (WHO, 2002). It includes promotion, prevention and restoring of wellbeing. A according to WHO, "there is no health without mental health" (2018), since mental health is a fundamental component of being healthy. It is defined as "a state of wellbeing, in which the individual realises his or her own abilities, can cope with the normal stresses of life, can work productively and fruitfully, and is able to make a contribution to his or her community" (WHO, 2018b). Therefore, it incorporates self-awareness of individuals' strengths, resources and an ability to use them to protect us against succumbing to adversity or help us promptly and effectively restore wellbeing afterwards. However, this is just one, perspective on wellbeing coming from a medical standpoint.

Another perspective comes from philosophy, which differentiates between hedonic and eudaemonic wellbeing (Burke, 2017). Hedonic wellbeing is about happiness, living a life full of pleasure. In contrast, eudaemonic wellbeing is a deeper-level wellbeing that incorporates life purpose, morality and meaning. Psychologists took these two philosophical perspectives and turned them into psychological theories by breaking them down into behaviours and attitudes and finding measures, as well as interventions that are designed to increase our wellbeing. Subsequently, two main models of wellbeing were created in psychology: (1) Subjective Wellbeing (otherwise known as hedonic wellbeing), emotional wellbeing, both simply referred to as happiness and (2) Psychological Wellbeing which is aligned with eudaemonia and represent a deeper-level wellbeing.

In addition to these main paradigms of wellbeing, we also have students' views on how they conceptualise it. While these views have not been incorporated into wellbeing models, they offer an invaluable insight into how a lay person sees their own wellbeing. This is particularly salient in the context of schools, in which wellbeing is freely practiced. Not surprisingly, young people find it difficult to define wellbeing, even though they are cognisant of what it means to them personally (Powell et al., 2018). They perceive wellbeing in the context of "being," "having," and "doing" it. A state of "being" refers to a situation, in which students' needs are met, they feel satisfied, happy, loved, connected, and hopeful. Being well means that they have trusting relationships with adults and peers, they are physically well, feel safe and are visible to others, in other words, their peers notice them.

The concept of "having" wellbeing was explained by young people as having the support of teachers and peers in relation to school work, equality, justice, and fairness. They have their say in school procedures, and the intricacies and differences in students' views are being considered by school leaders and teachers. They are respected and supported fully, especially in situations when they feel "stuck" and need help with learning. Another factor that they mentioned as important was the right to privacy, as sometimes they felt that the educational system and electronic monitoring was set up in a way that infringed on their right to privacy. This included confiscating phones, teachers' access to personal information, as well as lack of physical privacy, an exclusive space in schools, where they can "hide" without their teachers watching them.

"Doing" wellbeing referred to students looking after themselves. This included being able to walk away from bullies, when they were hurting, learning to accept oneself with all their peculiarities, or an ability to make their own decisions in relation to who they want to be friends with or what goals they want to set up for themselves. In other words, they asked for a level of autonomy to be granted to them, and an opportunity to develop their skills and character. All these three dimensions of wellbeing as perceived by young people match the research in positive psychology, in relation to how wellbeing is defined. Even though students were unable to define it, their description and the explanation they have offered has a universal meaning.

More importantly, however, it is something that can easily be included in the school's wellbeing strategy to enhance students' conditions and in turn lead to improvement of their wellbeing.

In this book, wellbeing is defined as a journey of promoting and improving individuals' mental health and conditions, so that they can contribute to the school communities' overall wellbeing, and vice versa. Therefore, the same way as the individual's changes in attitude and behaviour have a domino-effect on the community's wellbeing, the wellbeing initiatives introduced in the school community, as planned in the school's wellbeing strategy, have a significant impact on individual's wellbeing. Together, the power of the individual with and within the community is what the school wellbeing is all about.

Context is everything

We all have a tendency to underestimate the situational factors that affect people (Ross, 1977). When we explain why Johnny hit Frank in the school yard, or why Tracy stole a sandwich from Mary, the first thing that pops into our mind is the perpetrators' stable characteristics, such as Johnny is always aggressive, and Tracy is greedy. Only then, we start considering the circumstances that may have affected their behaviour. Perhaps Frank told Johnny mean things about his sister for the tenth time this week, and Johnny could not take this harassment anymore, which is why he has resolved to violence. Equally, perhaps Tracy was hungry, as she had missed her breakfast this morning and saw Mary throwing her sandwich out every day, which is why she stole it from her before it ended up in the bin. The situational factors, in these examples, may not excuse Johnny's and Tracy's behaviour, but they have certainly contributed to it.

Wellbeing initiatives are similar, in that the majority of them make individuals responsible for their own wellbeing. Even though the researchers and practitioners call for interventions that target groups or communities (Seligman and Csikszentmihalyi, 2000), they are relatively rare. Given that students do not live in vacuum and the school and home environment affects them every day, it is crucial that we consider this angle when designing a wellbeing strategy for schools.

Physical environment

A few years ago I was invited to a secondary school to share with students some tips about enhancing their wellbeing. As I walked through the classroom door, I was struck by all the *positive* messages on the wall. They were happy, smiley faces all around me on the wall, stories of people who experienced hardship and didn't let it knock them down, the words "happy," "happiness" and "positivity" must have come up at least 50 times in the quotes around me. As I stood there in the middle of the room, I felt very uneasy. The teachers apparently called it a *happy room*, yet I bet students were sneering at it, as it must have been less than helpful for some of them.

When psychologists tried to identify the impact of *happy places* on our psyche, they carried out an experiment with a group of adults, who were asked to complete an anagram in a room filled with motivational posters and books (McGuirk et al., 2018). When individuals were able to do it, they felt highly motivated and more positive than they had before. After all, the posters have reaffirmed how happy and resilient they were. However, when they didn't do well in the anagram test, they felt more like a failure. This study showed that these happy spaces, as good as they sound, might not be so good for everyone, and not in all circumstances. They are great, when everything is going well for us, but as soon as we start facing challenges, we begin to compare ourselves to those who have apparently overcome their adversity so easily, and we feel that we are simply not good enough to do the same. This is why, the physical space of the classroom or our schools needs to be carefully thought through, and if it is too *happy*, perhaps it is a good idea to tone it down a little.

Another example of the impact of a physical space on students is the extent of noise we experience in school. Noise pollution has become an ever-increasing product of our complex habitat and is caused not only by technology but also by overcrowding (Firdaus, 2018). In schools with overcrowded classrooms, or an audible traffic-noise, students' wellbeing is significantly lower than in schools with lower levels of noise pollution (Scannell et al., 2016). Therefore, no matter how many wellbeing interventions we introduce, they might not be effective, if students' basic needs are not met. Instead of investing money in expensive wellbeing programmes, perhaps provisions should be made to reduce noise levels in a school. This could be part of your school's wellbeing strategy and may prove more effective in enhancing wellbeing than psycho-social interventions.

Major organisations, such as Google and Facebook, are known for putting effort into designing an optimal environment for their employees. They may be doing it partially to stand out from the crowd, but also, because the space in which we work and learn has an impact on our wellbeing. Research indicates that in schools, what matters is the level of lighting and colours that are warm and inviting. A also the act of opening the schools to the community after hours, so that students want to stay on and enjoy the communal space, amplifies their school-belonging (Walden, 2009). This brings us to the "feel" of the schools, whereby the presence of soft furnishing around the building is associated with increases of students' comfort during long hours of sitting in the classroom (Wingrat and Exner, 2005). Subliminally, it sends a message to students that teachers and leaders care about them enough to do it and want them to linger in their school and catch up with friends after classes.

Another example of an optimal wellbeing-enhancing design is providing students with spaces that offer them some natural views (Benfield et al., 2015), so that they can practice sky-gazing, which is an up-and-coming wellbeing intervention (Conway and Hefferon, forthcoming) Other physical environment factors include good air circulation, so that they don't feel exhausted breathing excessive CO_2 which can make them sleepy at the end of each class, or adequate temperature, so that they don't have to put on additional layers, or take jumpers off, which some teachers don't even allow them to do, as they see it disrespectful (Salthammer et al., 2016). All these factors are just as important for enhancing students' wellbeing and are worthy of being put in the school's wellbeing strategy, as are the wellbeing programmes and interventions designed to directly boost their wellbeing.

There are still many schools in developed countries that do not have access to warm water, meaning that students wash their hands under a cold tap and schools that send their children home when the temperature drops below zero degrees Celsius, because they cannot afford adequate heating system. This is something that governments who set up the guidelines for wellbeing should look at first, before they ask teachers and school leaders to introduce wellbeing programmes and interventions in school. After all, following Maslow's Hierarchy of Needs (Maslow, 1958), our physical needs come before intellectual ones, and it is crucial we consider them, as they may impact not only on students' physical wellbeing but also their attitude towards learning.

School climate

I was once invited to a secondary school to give a talk to students about wellbeing. A few minutes into my talk, I noticed a commotion in the back. Apparently, one of the students said a rude word to another, and the teacher sitting in the back overhead them and interrupted my talk explaining that I need to hold off until she fetches the principal and gets this situation sorted. As we waited for the teacher to return, I tried to chit-chat with the students but they were not very talkative, just looked around grimly and kept quiet. Five minutes later, three ladies walked in, a teacher present at my talk, another teacher who was responsible for school's wellbeing, and the third person who was the school leader. They all stood three in a row next to me, as the leader was wagging her finger aggressively at students, and berating all children by saying that this nice lady (me) came to the school to offer them some wise advice on how to enhance their wellbeing and instead of being grateful, they have *shamed* the school.

I stood there completely astounded about the overreaction of the teaching staff to a relatively small incident. My heart went out to the children, many of whom sat with their heads hanging, even though they had nothing to do with the commotion that happened there earlier. I tried to intervene and say that it was not a big deal, but the school leader cut me off half-way through the sentence, and once I was put firmly in my box, she continued with her monologue. The rest of my session went on with a cloud of sadness over all our heads, and an understandable lack of engagement from students. They were only 12 years old, in their first year of secondary school and they had already experienced shameless behaviour not from other kids, but the teaching staff who may have talked the talk of wellbeing, but certainly did not walk the walk. I know that this incident is unusual and most school staff would be appalled by this behaviour, but it did not seem unusual to the teachers standing there before the children, and the young people who were possibly exposed to it daily.

Wellbeing starts in the staff room – they say, and having visited various schools over the years, I concur. At this point, judging from the attitude of a school leader, I can (usually) accurately predict the behaviour of both teachers and students in their schools. When the school leader does not treat their staff with respect, the same lack of value for human beings is usually seen across the board (Randle-Robins, 2016). Conversely, when the leader shows trust and kindness, regardless of what type of school I am visiting, the students and teachers in this school tend to live by similar values. This is why, in my opinion, actions to enhance the dignity and respect for all members of the school community should be a part of the school's wellbeing strategy.

There are countries where the ministers of education introduced policies according to which school wellbeing needs to become part of the school curriculum. When assessing the adherence to the policy, many school inspectors focus on the artificial data, such as what programmes were implemented, who delivered them, and for how many hours? They focus on the tangible information that quite frankly sometimes does not match the reality. The school I mentioned above would have ticked off all the boxes for implementing wellbeing, yet they did not practice it every day. Therefore, changes need to be made on an inspectorate level to consider the nuances of the impact of the school ethos on a school community's wellbeing.

The practice of wellbeing is about instilling values that everyone, regardless of their role, re-enacts in their school. Often, it is the board of management, patronage or school leader that decides upon it, and it is then reflected in the standards set up at the recruitment stage of the school staff, thus it permeates into the classroom. Sometimes, however, it is the school community that decides upon it and the leader becomes a gate keeper for the values which are lived daily. What the leader does, and what behaviours and attitude they promote or frown upon in their school makes the school culture come alive.

A leader of a large secondary school once told me a story about one of her teachers, let's call her Alice, who suffers from depression. Many years ago, Alice had a serious depressive episode, leaving her sick and in need of hospitalisation for over six months. In order to prevent a similar incident from happening again, the leader agreed with the teacher that in the future, before she spirals down, she should go to her and tell her when she does not feel well. This way, the leader was protecting Alice from experiencing yet another episode of illness, as well as protecting young people from the potential effects of their teachers' depressive episode. Like the rest of the staff, now Alice trusts her leader fully and, in turn, her kind and fair leader is able to manage her school more effectively in full knowledge of what is happening in each one of her staff members' lives that may have impact on the school. This mutual respect helps all involved and is a great example of how wellbeing can come from not only a structured intervention, but the culture of an organisation and its practice.

Creating a climate of wellbeing is of upmost importance for students and staff. There is no point in *talking* about it, if we are not *walking* it. Dignity at work ensures that people are treated with utmost respect and in a way that is conducive to their wellbeing. A positive school climate has a significant impact on our wellbeing (Aldridge and McChesney, 2018). The good thing is that it is the individuals who create a wellbeing climate in their schools, not the building nor the policy. This means that even if it is not working well for you at the moment, the culture, as much as people's attitudes can change. Here are five areas that schools need to focus on to enhance their school climate: (1) safety, physical and socio-emotional; (2) relationships, accepting diversity and nurturing relations that provide support; (3) teaching and learning, offering help to all students; (4) school physical environment; (5) the process of improvement of school climate (Thapa et al., 2012). If part of the school's wellbeing strategy was to address some of these points, it could have a positive effect on the entire school community's wellbeing.

Teachers wellbeing

A few years ago, I was visiting a primary school. It is based in an old convent with high ceilings, large windows and long corridors. As I was walking down the corridor filled with the smell of hot-lunch in the air and the cheerful sound of excited pupils about to have their long break, the proud school leader was walking by my side showcasing the wonderful initiatives they have implemented for their children. She pointed to the large noticeboards with a lot of uplifting messages, a gratitude wall and a recent wellbeing award they had received. I was very impressed and enjoyed listening to the inspirational things that the adult community have done for their children. As we were coming to the end of my visit, I commended her on the work that the wellbeing team have done to make pupils' lives better and asked what they have done for their teachers. I was met with a short silence and then a quick: *We're working on it* response.

We cannot talk about ways of enhancing students' wellbeing without firstly talking about their teachers. Teachers' and students' wellbeing is interconnected and interdependent. In a study with 25 schools, 3,215 students and 1,182 teachers in the UK, the results showed that when teachers boasted high levels of wellbeing, their students reported similar results (Harding et al., 2019). Worryingly, however, when teachers reported having symptoms of depression, such as negative thoughts, negative feelings, suicidal ideations, exhaustion, began to lose or gain weight, or complained of disturbed sleep, their students reported higher levels of psychological distress and poorer levels of wellbeing. Students' and teachers' wellbeing are part of one educational ecosystem.

Are you surprised with these findings? Most educational professionals are not. After all, we do have scientific evidence to suggest that our happiness is contagious (Fowler and Christakis, 2009). A longitudinal study that followed almost 5,000 individuals over 20 years found that when one person in a social network becomes happier (e.g., due to marriage, winning the lottery, falling in love, or experiencing another reason for good fortune), it has a knock-on effect on other people in their network, even those who didn't have a direct contact with that person. Happiness extends to three degrees of separation. When our immediate friends became happier, it has a 15% impact on our happiness. When their friends became happier, it has a 10% impact on our happiness. And if friends of those friends became happier, it has a 5.6% impact on our own happiness. The proximity of happier people has the highest effect, which is why if a friend who lives within a mile-radius from us and becomes happier it increases the probability of our own happiness by 25%, whereas our next-door neighbours' happiness boosts our wellbeing by 34%. This study illustrates how surrounding ourselves with people who are psychologically and emotionally well can enhance our own wellbeing. Imagine the effect that wellbeing-enhancing changes in your school could potentially have on your entire school community.

This contagious trend is not limited to a face-to-face interaction, as it is also noted in online interplay (Coviello et al., 2014), such as online learning. This is particularly important in a post-COVID education system. The analysis of social networks over a 3-year period found that when there was rainfall in one part of the world, it not only reduced the wellbeing of people living there, but had a subsequently negative effect on their online social network. The reason for it maybe because we tend to "leak" our emotional state through the words we use, and the topics we choose to discuss. These nuances are easily picked up by others, who might not be conscious of them, yet their moods have somewhat affected them. This is why regardless of whether we are teaching face-to-face or online, teachers' and the entire school community's wellbeing, including parents, is important to put in the school's wellbeing strategy.

Children are affected not only by teachers' moods and their mental state, but also by the relationship they have with their educators. In a study with students who completed a tactile task that allowed them to describe what wellbeing meant to them, students found that their positive description of school was associated with supportive teachers, who provided them with creative ways to learn and listened to their ideas and concerns (Huynh and Stewart-Tufescu, 2019). On the other hand, when the school caused them grief and dissatisfaction which resulted in lower levels of wellbeing, their artwork described unsupportive teachers who were not tuned into what they thought or felt. Teachers, therefore, were at the forefront of students' wellbeing.

Apart from the impact of unhappy teachers on students, another reason as to why we should start with the wellbeing of our teachers is because when individuals are experiencing symptoms of depression, anxiety and other mental health issues, their thoughts, feelings, and behaviours alter (Innstrand et al., 2012). They may become more irritable, thus raising their voice at students or snapping at them. They may become less patient and as such punish students for behaviours they would have ignored otherwise. They also may become more self-focussed, thus not noticing what is happening to students and how they can help them. In general, teachers living a healthier lifestyle had a higher level of quality teaching than those who did not (Boateng and Chirapanda, 2015). Therefore, their wellbeing needs to be put first, when designing a wellbeing strategy for school.

That said, it is challenging enough to implement wellbeing for students. Some may think that if we have to do the same for teachers, or the rest of the school community, it would take a lot of extra resources that schools do not have. Indeed, some schools offer programmes for teachers and school leaders such as *Progressive Muscle Relaxation* (Reynolds et al., 2020), *Mindfulness-based Stress Reduction* (Janssen et al., 2018), or *Cultivating Awareness and Resilience in Education* (Sharp and Jennings, 2016) and many more. They indeed require resources, unless they are funded by the organisers. However, our recent research shows us that these programmes are not required to put teachers' wellbeing first.

One of my doctoral students, Annemarie Doran, has been looking at wellbeing provision for teachers for the last few years. As part of her dissertation, she surveyed teachers to find out what environmental factors affected their personal levels of wellbeing. Her findings showed that what predicted their wellbeing was not the provision of a *wellbeing for teachers policy*, or schools organising wellbeing continuous professional development for educators, such as mindfulness or wellbeing programmes, rather (1) management showing that they care and (2) putting the support structures in place for teachers (Doran et al., forthcoming). All this taps into the basic needs of teachers who want to experience dignity at work and feel that the management cares. This is an easy intervention to implement as part of the school's wellbeing strategy that can bring so many personal benefits to all.

Apart from caring about our teachers and putting support structures in place, we can also use the whole series of free interventions that this book reviews in Chapters 3 and 4. Past research shows us that applying such interventions made teachers feel more calm and positive in the classroom (Turner and Theilking, 2019). They also reported being more engaged with teaching and noticed an improvement in their relationships with students. This, in turn, resulted in them being more sensitive to students' needs and in turn students' behaviour and attitude became more positive. Students of teachers who used these interventions provided them with more positive feedback, creating a positivity loop that made their lessons more engaging, deeper and meaningful. This is an example of how a small teacher intervention can ripple down and make a significant difference to the students and possibly the whole-school community.

There is yet another reason for the importance of focusing on teachers' wellbeing. According to some researchers, career wellbeing is the most influential component of overall wellbeing (Rath and Harter, 2010). This means that individuals who report high levels of career wellbeing are more than twice as likely to experience overall psychological wellbeing. This is consistent with longitudinal research suggesting that our life-span development is dwarfed when we don't take the time to advance our career-related skills (Vaillant, 2003). These findings are not surprising given that we spend a significant portion of our day at work. If we don't enjoy what we do, it will make it more challenging for us to feel fulfilled in life. Similarly, if we feel unhappy, it may affect people around us.

In this book, we will be discussing wellbeing from the students' perspective. A lot of the research presented in the book relates to the wellbeing of young people, although some of it is associated with adults. However, rest assured that apart from a few exceptions, the concepts relating to wellbeing are universal for people of all ages. Therefore, even though my focus when writing this book was on young people, these wellbeing interventions are perfect for teachers, leaders and other members of the school community, such as parents, patrons, board of directors. They can be implemented for individuals (e.g., identifying individual character strengths), for groups (identifying teachers' or a specific class' strengths), or the entire school or community (e.g., identifying the values we all live by). Each one of the interventions can be viewed from all these three perspectives, even though I write about them as an initiative for individuals. After all, increasingly the research suggests that the most effective wellbeing projects are the whole-school initiatives, in which wellbeing permeates through the entire community (Goldberg et al., 2019), allowing students to bask in wellness everywhere they go. This is why, as you are going through the remainder of this book, I encourage you to stop after each section and reflect on how you can use the knowledge you're reading about in your specific school context and with all the members of your school community.

The pedagogy of wellbeing

The focus of the current book is a creation of a wellbeing strategy based specifically on psycho-social interventions and programmes that intentionally enhance the school community's wellbeing. However, there is yet another, very important medium through which wellbeing can be introduced to students, and it relates to weaving wellbeing into the tapestry of the existing curriculum. It relates to both the content of the curriculum, as well as the delivery.

One of the ways in which wellbeing can be taught is by changing the lesson content (Seligman, 2011). English literature may include discussions about the meaning of kindness or gratitude, thus helping students ponder and percolate these concepts. Geography may include a discussion about the happiest countries around the world and pinpointing on the map where they are located. Therefore, it may become an integral part of what students are learning without specifically discussing with them what they need to do to enhance their wellbeing. This approach to wellbeing improvement should be integrated into the wellbeing strategy. All teachers may think, suggest and/or experiment with ways to tweak their lesson content to include wellbeing.

Wellbeing pedagogy also impacts on students via the quality of the student–teacher interaction. When teachers are asked about the sources of their own wellbeing, they do not mention any specific wellbeing programmes they attended, but the simple interactions with their students in socially and pedagogically challenging situations, which affected them positively or negatively (Soini et al., 2010). Equally for students, the interactions they had with their teachers and peers were the most powerful source of wellbeing (Pyhalto et al., 2010). This highlights the importance of the quality of teaching and learning, appropriate class management and the calibre of day-to-day interactions in schools, all of which have a powerful impact on wellbeing.

Our teaching practices also have a capacity to influence wellbeing. A couple of years ago, I came across a study demonstrating that giving students' long instructions to carry out an activity may have a negative effect on their wellbeing (Goemaere et al., 2018). When teachers' long and short instructions were compared it transpired that the longer the teachers' explanation was, the more it resulted in students' irritation and lower levels of their productivity and accuracy. I have been teaching for over 20 years and always wanted to make sure I was clear in my instructions, which is why I was possibly guilty of overly long instructions. Apologies to all my past students who are reading this book. I have since consciously thought of ways, in which I can reduce the level of detail I provide. After all, the last thing I would want is to negatively affect my students' wellbeing. This is just an example of how individual teaching techniques can be tweaked to boost our students' wellness. There are plenty more things we can do, but what is important is to be aware of it, reflect and change our practice when required.

The current book will provide some psycho-social tools that can be used by students and teachers on a daily basis. It will not cover the topic of the pedagogy of wellbeing, which is so vast that a separate book could be written about it. However, both the lesson-content changes that facilitate knowledge about wellbeing and the impact of the pedagogy on wellbeing should become an integral part of the school's wellbeing strategy, helping the community apply a truly whole-school approach.

Take-aways for the school's wellbeing strategy

- Students' levels of mental health issues continue to rise, so we need to do more or approach wellbeing in schools differently to tackle this problem head on.
- Wellbeing has a pejorative meaning and can be seen as wicked and/or harmful, if done incorrectly; and elusive, as it is so vast and encompasses various fields of science.
- This book focuses mainly on introducing psycho-social interventions in school.
- However, the context of school and home environment can have a negative impact on students, which is why it should become an integral part of the school's wellbeing strategy.

References

Aldridge, J. M. & Mcchesney, K. 2018. The relationships between school climate and adolescent mental health and wellbeing: A systematic literature review. *International Journal of Educational Research*, 88, 121–145.

Algoe, S. B., Fredrickson, B. L. & Gable, S. L. 2013. The social functions of the emotion of gratitude via expression. *Emotion*, 13, 605–609.

Bache, I., Reardon, L. & Anand, P. 2016. Wellbeing as a wicked problem: Navigating the arguments for the role of government. *Journal of Happiness Studies*, 17, 893–912.

Bale, C. & Mishara, B. 2004. Developing an International Mental Health Promotion Programme for Young Children. *International Journal of Mental Health Promotion*, 6, 12–16.

Benfield, J. A., Rainbolt, G. N., Bell, P. A. & Donovan, G. H. 2015. Classrooms with nature views: Evidence of differing student perceptions and behaviors. *Environment & Behavior*, 47, 140–157.

Binfet, J.-T. 2015. Not-so random acts of kindness: A guide to intentional kindness in the classroom. *International Journal of Emotional Education*, 7, 49–62.

Bloomfield, A. 2019. What does a wellbeing budget mean for health and health care? *Milbank Quarterly*, 97, 897–900.

Boateng, J. N. & Chirapanda, S. 2015. The well-being of foreign teachers in Bangkok schools and its impact on quality teaching. *UTCC International Journal of Business & Economics*, 7, 149–171.

Brown, B. 2012. *Daring Greatly How the Courage to Be Vulnerable Transforms the Way We Live, Love, Parent, and Lead*. New York: Gotham Books.

Burke, J. 2017. *Happiness after 30: The Paradox of Aging*. Dublin: Jumpp Publishing.

Burke, J. 2018. Conceptual framework for a positive psychology coaching practice. *Coaching Psychologist*, 14, 16–25.

Burke, J. & Minton, S. J. 2019. Well-being in post-primary schools in Ireland: The assessment and contribution of character strengths. *Irish Educational Studies*, 38, 177–192.

Conway, P. & Hefferon, K. forthcoming. The extraordinary in the ordinary: Skychology – An interpretative phenomenological analysis of looking up at the sky.

Costello, E. J., Mustillo, S., Erkanli, A., Keeler, G. & Angold, A. 2003. Prevalence and development of psychiatric disorders in childhood and adolescence. *Archives of General Psychiatry*, 60, 837–844.

Coviello, L., Sohn, Y., Kramer, A. D. I., Marlow, C., Franceschetti, M., Christakis, N. A. & Fowler, J. H. 2014. Detecting emotional contagion in massive social networks. *PLoS ONE*, 9, 1–6.

Deshea, L. 2003. A scenario-based scale of willingness to forgive. *Individual Differences Research*, 1, 201–217.

Doran, A., Burke, J. & Healy, C. forthcoming. *The influence of school leaders on teachers' personal wellbeing*.

EDUCATION.IE. 2019. *Wellbeing policy statement and framework for practice*. Dublin, Ireland.

Emmons, R. A. & Mccullough, M. E. 2003. Counting blessings versus burdens: An experimental investigation of gratitude and subjective well-being in daily life. *Journal of Personality and Social Psychology*, 84, 377–389.

Firdaus, G. 2018. Increasing rate of psychological distress in urban households: How does income matter? *Community Mental Health Journal*, 54, 641–648.

Fitzpatrick, K. & Tinning, R. 2014. Health education's fascist tendencies: A cautionary exposition. *Critical Public Health*, 24, 132–142.

Fowler, J. H. & Christakis, N. A. 2009. Dynamic spread of happiness in a large social network: Longitudinal analysis over 20 years in the Framingham Heart Study. *BMJ: British Medical Journal*, 338, 1–13.

Fredrickson, B. L., Tugade, M. M. & Waugh, C. E. 2003. What good are positive emotions in crises? A prospective study of resilience and emotions following the terrorist attacks on the United States on September 11th, 2001. *Journal of Personality & Social Psychology*, 84, 365–376.

Fredrickson, B. L., Cohn, M. A., Coffey, K. A., Pek, J. & Finkel, S. M. 2008. Open hearts build lives: Positive emotions, induced through loving-kindness meditation, build consequential personal resources. *Journal of Personality and Social Psychology*, 95, 1045–1062.

Goemaere, S., Beyers, W., de Muynck, G.-J. & Vansteenkiste, M. 2018. The paradoxical effect of long instructions on negative affect and performance: When, for whom and why do they backfire? *Acta Astronautica*, 147, 421–430.

Goldberg, J. M., Sklad, M., Elfrink, T. R., Schreurs, K. M. G., Bohlmeijer, E. T. & Clarke, A. M. 2019. Effectiveness of interventions adopting a whole school approach to enhancing social and emotional development: A meta-analysis. *European Journal of Psychology of Education – EJPE*, 34, 755–782.

GOV.UK. 2013. National wellbeing [Online]. Available: https://www.gov.uk/government/collections/national-wellbeing [Accessed on 23rd Sep 2020].

GOV.UK. 2018. Mental health of children and young people in England, 2017 [Online]. Available: https://digital.nhs.uk/data-and-information/publications/statistical/mental-health-of-children-and-young-people-in-england/2017/2017 [Accessed on 23rd Sep 2020].

Harding, S., Morris, R., Gunnell, D., Ford, T., Hollingworth, W., Tilling, K., Evans, R., Bell, S., Grey, J., Brockman, R., Campbell, R., Araya, R., Murphy, S. & Kidger, J. 2019. Is teachers' mental health and wellbeing associated with students' mental health and wellbeing? *Journal of Affective Disorders*, 253, 460–466.

Harford, T. 2019. Why happiness is easy to venerate and hard to generate? *Financial Times [Online]*. Available: https://www.ft.com/content/7f73002a-3a95-11e9-b856-5404d3811663. [Accessed on 23rd Sep 2020].

Hay, L. 1984. *You Can Heal Your Life*. Carlsbad, CA: Hay House Inc.

Howell, A. 2017. Self-affirmation theory and the science of well-being. *Journal of Happiness Studies: An Interdisciplinary Forum on Subjective Well-Being*, 18, 293–311.

Huynh, E. & Stewart-Tufescu, A. 2019. 'I get to learn more stuff': Children's understanding of wellbeing at School in Winnipeg, Manitoba, Canada. *International Journal of Emotional Education*, 11, 84–96.

Innstrand, S. T., Langballe, E. M. & Falkum, E. 2012. A longitudinal study of the relationship between work engagement and symptoms of anxiety and depression. *Stress & Health: Journal of the International Society for the Investigation of Stress*, 28, 1–10.

Janssen, M., Heerkens, Y., Kuijer, W., van der Heijden, B. & Engels, J. 2018. Effects of mindfulness-based stress reduction on employees' mental health: A systematic review. *PLoS ONE*, 13, 1–37.

Kroll, C. & Delhey, J. 2013. A happy nation? Opportunities and challenges of using subjective indicators in policymaking. *Social Indicators Research*, 114, 13–28.

Lyubomirsky, S. 2007. *The How of happiness: A Scientific Approach to Getting the Life You Want*. New York: Penguin Press.

Lyubomirsky, S., Sheldon, K. M. & Schkade, D. 2005. Pursuing happiness: The architecture of sustainable change. *Review of General Psychology*, 9, 111–131.

Maslow, A. H. 1958. A dynamic theory of human motivation. In: Stacey, C. L. & Demartino, M. (eds.), *Understanding Human Motivation*. Cleveland, OH: Howard Allen Publishers.

Mcguirk, L., Kuppens, P., Kingston, R. & Bastian, B. 2018. Does a culture of happiness increase rumination over failure? *Emotion*, 18, 755–764.

Murphy, G. & Baines, J. 2015. Connecting the dots: Facilitating a positive university educational journey with an organisational mental health and wellbeing strategy. *Journal of the Australian & New Zealand Student Services Association*, 46, 20–27.

Oliver, S., Harden, A., Rees, R., Shepherd, J., Brunton, G. & Oakley, A. 2008. Young people and mental health: Novel methods for systematic review of research on barriers and facilitators. *Health Education Research*, 23, 770–790.

Powell, M. A., Graham, A., Fitzgerald, R., Thomas, N. & White, N. E. 2018. Wellbeing in schools: What do students tell us? *Australian Educational Researcher*, 45, 515–531.

Pyhalto, K., Soini, T. & Pietarinen, J. 2010. Pupils' pedagogical well-being in comprehensive school – Significant positive and negative school experiences of Finnish ninth graders. *European Journal of Psychology of Education*, 25, 207–221.

Quinn, P., McGilloway, S. & Burke, J. 2020. "The Class of 2020": The experience of Leaving Certificate students during COVID-19 in Ireland. Maynooth: Maynooth University.

Randle-Robins, E. 2016. *The Hands-On Guide to School Improvement: Transform Culture, Empower Teachers, and Raise Student Achievement.* Golden Valley, MN: Free Spirit Publishing.

Rath, T. & Harter, J. 2010. *Wellbeing: The Five Essential Elements.* New York: Gallup Pr.

Reynolds, L. W., Bruno, A. J., Ross, K. M., Hall, J. M. & Reynolds, J. 2020. Bolstering staff wellbeing in schools. *Journal of School Health*, 90, 425–428.

Richter, L. M., Daelmans, B., Lombardi, J., Heymann, J., Boo, F. L., Behrman, J. R., Lu, C., Lucas, J. E., Perez-Escamilla, R., Dua, T., Bhutta, Z. A., Stenberg, K., Gertler, P. & Darmstadt, G. L. 2017. Advancing early childhood development: From science to Scale 3: Investing in the foundation of sustainable development: Pathways to scale up for early childhood development. *The Lancet*, 389, 103–118.

Ross, L. 1977. The intuitive psychologist and his shortcomings: Distortions in the attribution process. *Advances in Experimental Social Psychology*, 10, 173–220.

Salthammer, T., Uhde, E., Schripp, T., Schieweck, A., Morawska, L., Mazaheri, M., Clifford, S., He, C., Buonanno, G., Querol, X., Viana, M. & Kumar, P. 2016. Children's well-being at schools: Impact of climatic conditions and air pollution. *Environment International*, 94, 196–210.

Scannell, L., Hodgson, M., García Moreno Villarreal, J. & Gifford, R. 2016. The role of acoustics in the perceived suitability of, and well-being in, informal learning spaces. *Environment & Behavior*, 48, 769–795.

Seligman, M. E. P. 2011. *Flourish: A Visionary New Understanding of Happiness and Well-Being.* New York: Atria.

Seligman, M. E. P. & Csikszentmihalyi, M. 2000. Positive psychology: An introduction. *American Psychologist*, 55, 5–14.

Sharp, J. E. & Jennings, P. A. 2016. Strengthening teacher presence through mindfulness: What educators say about the Cultivating Awareness and Resilience in Education (CARE) program. *Mindfulness*, 7, 209–218.

Shrivastava, S. R., Shrivastava, P. S., Ramasamy, J. & Gnanavel, S. 2015. Necessity of globally implementing the comprehensive mental health action plan: World Health Organization. *Journal of Neurosciences in Rural Practice*, 6, 626–628.

Soini, T., Pyhalto, K. & Pietarinen, J. 2010. Pedagogical well-being: Reflecting learning and well-being in teachers' work. *Teachers and Teaching: Theory and Practice*, 16, 735–751.

Svane, D., Evans, N. & Carter, M.-A. 2019. Wicked wellbeing: Examining the disconnect between the rhetoric and reality of wellbeing interventions in schools. *Australian Journal of Education*, 63, 209–231.

Thapa, A., Cohen, J., Higgins-D'Alessandro, A., Guffey, S. & National School Climate, C. 2012. School climate research summary: August 2012. *School Climate Brief, Number 3*. New York: National School Climate Center.

Turner, K. & Theilking, M. 2019. Teacher wellbeing: Its effects on teaching practice and student learning. *Issues in Educational Research*, 29, 938–960.

UN. 2020. What is the International Day of Happiness? [Online]. Available: https://www.un.org/en/observances/happiness-day [Accessed].

UNESCO. 2016. UNESCO strategy on: Education for health and well-being: Contributing to the sustainable development of goals. Paris, France.

UNICEF. 2016. Strategy for health: 2016–2030. New York.

Vaillant, G. E. 2003. *Aging Well: Surprising Guideposts to a Happier Life*. New York: Little, Brown.

Walden, R. 2009. *Schools for the Future: Design Proposals from Architectural Psychology*. Ashland, OH: Hogrefe & Huber Publishers.

WHO. 2002. Constitution of the World Health Organization. *Bulletin of the World Health Organization*, 80, 983–984.

WHO. 2014. *Mental health: A state of wellbeing* [Online]. Available: https://www.who.int/features/factfiles/mental_health/en/ [Accessed on 23rd Sep 2020].

WHO. 2018a. *Adolescent mental health* [Online]. Available: https://www.who.int/mental_health/maternal-child/adolescent/en/ [Accessed on 23rd Sep 2020].

WHO. 2018b. *Fact sheets on sustainable development goals: Health targets – Mental Health*. Available: http://www.euro.who.int/__data/assets/pdf_file/0017/348011/Fact-sheet-SDG-Mental-health-UPDATE-02-05-2018.pdf?ua=1.

WHO. 2019. *Child and adolescent mental health [Online]*. Available: https://www.who.int/mental_health/maternal-child/child_adolescent/en/#:~:text=Worldwide%2010%2D20%25%20of%20children,young%20people%20in%20all%20regions. [Accessed on 23rd Sep 2020].

Wigford, A. & Higgins, A. 2019. Wellbeing in international schools: Teachers' perceptions. *Educational & Child Psychology*, 36, 46–64.

Wingrat, J. K. & Exner, C. E. 2005. The impact of school furniture on fourth grade children's on-task and sitting behavior in the classroom: A pilot study. *Work*, 25, 263–272.

Wood, J. V., Perunovic, W. Q. E. & Lee, J. W. 2009. Positive self-statements: Power for some, peril for others. *Psychological Science*, 20, 860–866.

World Health Organisation. 2018. *Mental health: Strengthening our response [Online]*. Available: https://www.who.int/news-room/fact-sheets/detail/mental-health-strengthening-our-response [Accessed on 23rd Sep 2020].

CHAPTER 2

Making sense of the complex world of wellbeing

Ill-being vs wellbeing

The most prominent, contemporary and widespread conceptualisation of wellbeing comes from the dual continua model of mental health, according to which, mental health and mental illness are related, but constitute two different dimensions that influence each other over our lifespan (Westerhof and Keyes, 2010). Traditionally, the absence of mental illness was perceived as mental health, which is why in situations such as school bullying, some students were incorrectly seen as unaffected by violence for as long as they had not developed pathologies, such as depression or anxiety (Burke and Minton, 2016). While common sense tells us it is not an accurate approach, it has existed for a long time, until the first model of duality of mental health was published in late 1990s (Tudor, 1996), and further developed in the 2000s (Keyes, 2002).

According to the model, mental health is on a continuum between (1) mental illness, through to (2) languishing, (3) having moderate mental health and (4) exceptional mental health (flourishing). Languishing is a state preceding mental illness diagnosis, whereby we experience some symptoms of mental illness but not enough to be diagnosed. It is a tricky place to be in, as we don't quite know why we feel so "flat". In a way, a diagnosis helps us explain our emotional state and take action towards improving our health. When we experience languishing, the risk of developing a major depressive disorder within the next 12 months is sixfold compared to those who are flourishing. Until this model was developed, people who languished, experienced moderate and exceptional health were categorised as being well, which is a very simplistic perspective on wellbeing.

Given the spectrum of mental health and illness, wellbeing strategy set up for schools needs to address all groups of students, not only those who are not doing well. Therefore, some interventions may be introduced to help young people with mental illness, for example, depression, anxiety, self-harm, eating disorders and similar. They represent approximately 10–15% of the school population. In addition to this, students who are languishing (usually approx. 10%) may benefit from gaining an awareness of the state they are in, and finding practical ways to enhance their wellbeing in order to move into the group of the majority of the population who are moderately well. Equally, we must not forget about those who are doing well (approx. 50-60%), as they can always continue to develop their wellbeing skills to serve them well in stressful times. Finally, the group of flourishing students could become champions of wellbeing, but they can also learn other techniques for maintaining their wellbeing as there are many different aspects of wellness. Even though someone may score as flourishing in one model of wellbeing, they may not be flourishing when other aspects of wellbeing are considered. This is why it is crucial to design a school's wellbeing strategy that represents all levels of the school community's wellbeing and incorporates various components.

Componential wellbeing

There are hundreds of wellbeing models and frameworks around the world, which makes the field of wellbeing a little confusing. The predominant framework for understanding wellbeing from the philosophical and psychological perspectives is viewing it as hedonic or eudaemonic wellbeing (Disabato et al., 2016). Hedonic wellbeing refers to seeking the life of pleasure, whereas eudaemonic wellbeing is about deeper-level wellbeing, such as living a meaningful life, full of purpose, where pleasure is not an important consideration. The difference between philosophy and psychology is that philosophers came up with these two overarching concepts, whereas psychologists broke them all down into components that they tried to measure, which have ultimately become the wellbeing models applied in schools.

What all the current models have in common is that they are componential in nature. This means that wellbeing models have been created that consist of components of what the authors of the models believe constitutes wellbeing. Drawing from philosophy, psychology, sociology, anthropology and other fields. For instance, a Subjective Wellbeing (SWB) model follows the paradigm of hedonic wellbeing and consists of three components: (1) higher levels of positive emotions, (2) lower level of negative emotions and (3) life satisfaction (Diener, 1984). Therefore, the creators of the SWB model saw these three components as crucial for wellbeing. On the other hand, the Psychological Wellbeing (PWB) model follows the eudaemonic paradigm and consists of six components: (1) positive relations with others, (2) environmental mastery, (3) autonomy, (4) a feeling of life purpose, (5) self-acceptance and (6) personal growth. The creator of the model saw the SWB model as well as the whole concept of happiness it represents as too simplistic to describe the serious matter of wellbeing (Ryff, 1989).

For decades, these two models were compared and contrasted causing a bit of a chaos in the field of wellbeing, as scientists could not agree on which model to select. With the rise of positive psychology, which is a movement created in the late 1990s, the objective of which was to focus the attention of researchers and practitioners on what makes life worth living (Peterson, 2006) and progress research in the field of wellbeing (Seligman and Csikszentmihalyi, 2000), these two diametrically different philosophical paradigms were combined in an explosion of wellbeing models. From the positive psychological perspective, they have become known as the models of flourishing. Flourishing represents the highest level of wellbeing that includes hedonic and eudaemonic perspectives. Therefore, when designing your school's wellbeing strategy, I recommend you consider these two approaches. However, in this book for the ease of understanding and consistency, I will refer to the wellbeing and flourishing models only as wellbeing models.

The components of the wellbeing models derive from various research findings in psychology and other fields over the years. Table 2.1 presents some of the main models along with their components.

The individual components of each model are usually evidence-based or claim to be evidence-based. However, the way evidence is used to design a model differs. For instance, the model of PWB has a strong theoretical basis and was generated by drawing from almost a century of psychological literature on wellbeing, such as the theories created by Abraham Maslow, Carl Jung or Carl Rogers (Ryff, 1989). On the other hand, the Subjective Wellbeing (SWB) model emerged from exploratory research (surveys with people) that aimed to identify what makes people happy (Diener et al., 1999). All other models have their own rationale, some of them are based or rigorous science, others may be convenient or applicable to a specific environment, for example, schools. Regardless of the rationale for combining a number of components together, what matters is that the components represent an evidence of positive functioning.

In addition to the psychological models detailed in the table, there are various models created by larger organisations, such as WHO, UNICEF. Also, many governments and minsters of education worldwide publish their own frameworks for wellbeing, which can be used in your school. Each one of these models is componential. Let me give you a few examples of how components are applied to create a wellbeing model or a framework. The Gallup organisation, which is famous for their claim of researching employees from 98% of countries worldwide, specialises in work-related research (Gallup, 2020). Therefore, their wellbeing model consists of five components: (1) career wellbeing, (2) social wellbeing, (3) financial wellbeing, (4) physical wellbeing and (5) community wellbeing (Rath and Harter, 2010). While social, physical and community wellbeing are frequently mentioned components in other wellbeing models, what differentiates them from others are the *career* and *financial* components, which relate to their area of research and interest. Coincidently, a longitudinal study corroborated that career wellbeing is indeed important (Vaillant, 2003). However, not many models include *career wellbeing* as one of their components.

One of the popular models of wellbeing was that created by the Action for Happiness, a wellbeing movement in the UK, according to which the pathways to happiness are reflected in an acronym GREAT DREAM, which consist of (1) Giving, (2) Relating, (3) Exercising, (4) Appreciating, (5) Trying out, (6) Direction, (7) Resilience, (8) Emotion, (9) Acceptance, (10) Meaning (AFH, 2020). Even though the model alludes to viewing wellbeing as a hedonic, pleasure-seeking action, in their model, they have also included some of the eudaemonic components, such as *meaning* and *acceptance*.

In Positive Education, which is the application of positive psychology in schools (Boniwell, 2013), the most prevalent is the PERMA model (Seligman, 2011). PERMA is yet another acronym consisting of five components: (1) Positive emotions, (2) Engagement, (3) Relationships, (4) Meaning, (5) Accomplishment. Please note that the reason for its salient application in education may be due to the popularity of the man who created it (Martin Seligman). Seligman established the positive

TABLE 2.1 Models of wellbeing

Model	Components
Subjective Wellbeing (Diener, 1984)	Reduction of negative emotions Increase of positive emotions Life satisfaction
Psychological Wellbeing (Ryff, 1989)	Autonomy Environmental mastery Personal growth Positive relations with others Purpose in life Self-acceptance
Authentic Happiness (Seligman, 2002)*	Life of pleasure Life of engagement Life of meaning
PERMA (Seligman, 2011)	Positive emotions Engagement Relationships Meaning Accomplishment

Mental Health Continuum (Keyes, 2002)	Emotional wellbeing
	  – Positive affect
	  – Life satisfaction
	Social wellbeing
	  – Social contribution
	  – Social integration
	  – Social actualisation
	  – Social acceptance
	  – Social coherence
	PWB
	  – Self-acceptance
	  – Environmental mastery
	  – Positive relations with others
	  – Autonomy
	  – Purpose in life

Public health (Huppert and So, 2013)	Positive appraisal
	  – Positive emotion
	  – Life satisfaction
	Positive characteristics
	  – Emotional stability
	  – Vitality
	  – Optimism
	  – Resilience
	  – Self-esteem
	Positive functioning
	  – Engagement
	  – Competence
	  – Meaning
	  – Positive relationship

(*Continued*)

TABLE 2.1 (*Continued*)

Model	Components
Flourishing model (Diener, 2010)	Competence
	Self-acceptance
	Meaning
	Relatedness
	Optimism
	Giving
	Engagement

* This model was replaced a decade later by the PERMA model (Seligman, 2011).

psychology movement (Seligman and Csikszentmihalyi, 2000), and he is often referred to as the father of positive psychology. However, this is just one of many models that can be applied in schools. What really matters when deciding on which framework/model of wellbeing your school can follow are your school-specific requirements.

In the same way that academics, organisations and governments have created their frameworks and models of wellbeing, I encourage you to do the same for your schools. Once you are familiar with the evidence-based components of other models, you can pick and choose the ones that are most applicable for your school community and you can also alter the language to suit it. You may select one of the existing models and add to it a component or two that you believe should be included. Alternatively, you can create a survey in your school that will identify which components your community would like included in their wellbeing framework.

Here are a few examples of how the PERMA model was tweaked in schools to make it more relevant to students. The PROSPER framework of wellbeing includes the following components: (P) Positivity, (R) Relationships, (O) Outcomes, (S) Strengths, (P) Purpose, (E) Engagement and (R) Resilience (Noble and McGrath, 2015). Therefore, the *meaning* component of PERMA was replaced with *purpose* and they have added two other components of *strengths* and *resilience* to it. Another, GSS model, sometimes referred to as FLOURISH, also replaced *meaning* with *purpose*, as well as added *positive health* highlighting the importance of developing a healthy body (Williams, 2011). Other models based on PERMA are PERMA-H, where *physical health* was added as an supplementary component to the original model (Lai et al., 2018), and EPOCH, which stands for (E) Engagement, (P) Perseverance, (O) Optimism, (C) Connectedness, and (H) Happiness (Kern et al., 2016). At first, the similarity between EPOCH and PERMA is not obvious, but the authors of the model admit it was inspired by PERMA. This is how schools and other practitioners all around the world create their own wellbeing models by taking one model and changing some aspects of it.

One of the advantages of taking on an existing model is that if it derives from the field of psychology, it usually comes with a measuring tool, otherwise referred to as either a scale, a test, or a questionnaire that we can use to assess the success of our wellbeing strategy and its application in school, which is important. This way, if you hope to enhance your students' engagement with school and extracurricular activities, you can measure their engagement at the beginning of the year, as well as at the end of the year, and see if there was any improvement in it. If you choose a model with a pre-existing measure (e.g., EPOCH), then your measurement will be relatively straightforward. If you choose to mix and match, you will need to use an additional measure to assess the components you have added.

Taking all this into consideration, there are no certain answers in the way we build models of wellbeing. All the current models of wellbeing consist of research-based components, and the components selected for each model are based on researchers' opinion as to what may potentially constitute wellbeing, rather than some universal truth. They also come with many limitations. This makes wellbeing relative, but therefore, offers schools an opportunity to create their own models relevant to their communities. Just like a "pick & mix" sweet shop, when creating a strategy for your school's wellbeing, you may either select an existing model, add to the existing model or choose the components that best suit your students and your school community.

Protective padding

When researchers reviewed longitudinal data from over 6,000 participants in the UK, they found that some people experienced high levels of wellbeing and low levels of ill-being, which is what we would expect from people who are flourishing. However, there was also a curious group of over 30% of people who have experienced both the symptoms of ill-being (e.g. anxiety) and the symptoms of wellbeing (scored high at some components of wellbeing) at the same time, meaning that mental illness and mental health may after all be independent from each other (Huppert and Whittington, 2003).

This is a fascinating phenomenon that also makes a lot of sense. Think of wellbeing as a *protective padding* that we develop in good times to keep us safe and warm in bad times. When we have high levels of self-esteem or positive emotions (components of wellbeing that act as a protective padding), we can bounce back from our adversities more effectively than when our self-esteem is low and we experience a lot of negative emotions (Tugade and Fredrickson, 2004). This is what happens to the people who have both symptoms of wellbeing and ill-being. Despite experiencing pathologies (e.g., depression, anxiety, self-harm, eating disorders), they may have also developed wellbeing skills (optimism, hope, effective coping) that help them deal with challenges in life. These skills, otherwise known as components of wellbeing, help them bounce back faster from adversity (Davidson and Begley, 2012), making them more resilient. This is ultimately the reason why we want to help our school community enhance their individual wellbeing components. Hopefully, they will serve as shields protecting them from depression, and other pathologies, when stressful times come, and also help those who are going through bad times build the strength to cope with their adversities effectively.

Wellbeing interventions

The good news is that regardless of what components you select for your school's wellbeing framework, there are possibly already some interventions or programmes that address them. A health intervention "is an act performed for, with or on behalf of a person or population whose purpose is to assess, improve, maintain, promote or modify health, functioning or health conditions" (WHO, 2017). As such, it covers a range of activities, some of which address a reduction in physical and mental health disorders, for example, depression, anxiety, self-harm or obesity, as well as an increase in the symptoms of wellbeing. In contrast, a wellbeing intervention, sometimes referred to as a positive psychology intervention, is an activity that aims to enhance individuals' positive emotions, positive thoughts or increase their positive behaviours (Sin and Lyubomirsky, 2009). While these types of interventions are also effective with clinical groups (Ruini and Fava, 2009), their main focus is to build positive elements of wellbeing (Parks and Biswas-Diener, 2013), such as our self-esteem, life satisfaction or happiness, of all those who are well. This book will discuss mainly the wellbeing interventions; however, the other side of the spectrum, that is, the reduction of disorders should also be considered when designing a school's wellbeing strategy.

Interventions we use can be evidence-based, evidence-informed or common-sense interventions. The evidence-based interventions are those that have been rigorously tested and have demonstrated that when applied our wellbeing is increased. Rigorous tests mean that they have been assessed with a group of people over a specific period of time. Their results are measured objectively with validated and reliable questionnaires and often compared to a control group that acts as a reference point for a change. Every experiment that tests the efficacy of an intervention has some limitations, be it the group is too small (usually approx. 30–60 people) or they have used a specific group of people, often college students to participate, who might not be the best representation of the population. However, despite these limitations, when individuals' wellbeing is increased as a result of participating in an experiment, it is deemed an evidence-based intervention, as we have some evidence that this specific intervention is effective in specific conditions. An example of such intervention is doing acts of kindness, which has been shown to enhance our wellbeing (Lyubomirsky et al., 2005).

When interventions are evidence-informed, it means that research suggests that the intervention may increase wellbeing, but it was not yet tested as part of an experiment. For example, one of my past students, Paul Conway, loves looking up into the sky, and as part of his master's degree he interviewed people who confirmed his assumption that sky-gazing enhances their self-reported wellbeing. Therefore, we have some evidence to suggest that when people look up into the sky for a period of time, it makes them feel better. However, we have not tested this idea yet; therefore, it is not yet based on evidence, but it is certainly an evidence-informed intervention. Carrying out an experimental study about sky-gazing in the future can be useful, as it may answer several questions we have about the effectiveness of this intervention and the mechanics of it. For instance, is gazing for a few seconds enough to boost our wellbeing, or do we need to spend at least half an hour looking up into the sky to see a lasting effect? Also, in what situations does it work best? What type of wellbeing does this intervention enhance, subjective or psychological? If it is psychological, what component in particular does it affect? These are some of the questions that researchers might address when assessing the effectiveness of this intervention in the future. Until then, sky-gazing is an evidence-informed activity.

Finally, we have common-sense interventions created by people who collect interventions from others or share with everyone what makes them feel good about living their lives to the full. For instance, my nana was one of the most elegant ladies I have ever met. I rarely saw her without a lipstick, high heels and even when sick, she made us put papillotes into her hair, so that she looked better the next day. She used to always say that when we feel down, all we need to do is put on an elegant outfit, and lipstick and even on the worst day, it will make us feel better. This is a common-sense intervention my nana has introduced into her life to enhance her own happiness. We now have researchers exploring this intervention and delving into the nuances of how our outfit impacts on our wellbeing (Smith, 2017). My granny didn't need any research to know it. For her, it was a common-sense intervention that kept her happy during the WW2 and beyond.

Common-sense interventions for enhancing wellbeing are important and useful for us, they are the folk wisdom that psychologists often tap into as the basis for their research, to identify evidence-informed and evidence-based activities. They should be cultivated in school by asking students questions to identify what it means for them to be happy and well, and let students come up with their own, common-sense interventions. That said, it would be useful to compliment them with some of the evidence-based and evidence-informed activities.

Many schools use this common-sense approach to enhance students' wellbeing. I recently explored this topic with 120 teachers asking them what they did in their schools to improve their students' wellbeing. Some of the ideas they shared included arranging an active homework on one day a week, themed weeks (e.g., various character strengths explored with students), games club, after-school interest classes, committees, positivity week, weekly assembly, where achievements are celebrated, class trips, guest-speakers from various wellbeing-related organisations, healthy eating classes and similar. Each one of these activities makes a lot of sense, even though we don't know for sure if they indeed enhance students' overall wellbeing. Yet, schools are intuitively doing them based on what they believe will make children happy. It is good to include such activities as part of the school's wellbeing strategy. What would make it even better is to assess their effectiveness using a well-established wellbeing assessment, as well as students' views.

Wellbeing programmes

A wellbeing programme is a group of interventions aimed at enhancing wellbeing. A few years ago, I was approached by a director of an organisation, who has read many positive psychology books and equipped with her newly gained knowledge, she designed a wellbeing programme for secondary school students. She asked me to evaluate it and I was happy to do it. However, I mentioned that if the random control trials indicate that the programme is not effective, she may need to alter its content to ensure it serves students. She was not happy to hear that, given that she had all the books for the programme printed out and some of them already delivered to schools. All she was looking for was a quality stamp from an academic to say that her programme was effective. After a long deliberation, she decided to decline my offer and the programme is now introduced in various schools and claims to enhance students' wellbeing, even though we have no such evidence as yet.

Many years ago, when I thought that it was better to introduce *any* wellbeing programme than no programme at all, a wise person asked me: *How do you know it does not harm children*? This question stayed with me for years, and since then I have been very cautious about introducing wellbeing in schools. As an academic, I have been working with many students who as part of their master's dissertation chose to either create or re-evaluate a wellbeing intervention or a programme. Regardless of how convincing the evidence for their effectiveness was, when introduced to a group of participants, some of these programmes did not enhance their wellbeing. Moreover, a few of them demonstrated a small negative impact on participants, such as enhanced stress levels or a reduction of job satisfaction, when they were carried out with teachers. Studies like these are common, and when they involve a re-evaluation of an existing programme, they are more likely to be published. Yet, when it is a newly designed programme, unless we see that there is some evidence that it works, a scientific journal might not be motivated enough to publish it creating a bias that doesn't allow us to see which combinations of components or activities do not work well. This is why it is crucial to evaluate your school's wellbeing strategy, including both students' views about the programme, and a validated measure of their wellbeing. This helps you make a decision as to what changes you can make to further enhance it.

A review of many health-promotion programmes has noted some similar negative effects on students' wellbeing (Griebler et al., 2017). Of 26 studies, six of them showed that some students felt ignored or not taken seriously enough when asked to participate in a programme. It is particularly frustrating for young people, when the programme content does not match their interests. Also, some students complained that wellbeing programmes were a distraction for them. For example, when they were asked to attend a programme during intense exam-preparation months, they saw it as a hindrance to them. Other studies reported a small increase of school bullying after the introduction of a series of wellbeing interventions (Weare and Nind, 2011). All these factors need to be considered when deciding on a wellbeing programme. This is why introducing any programme for the sake of it, in hope that it *surely* cannot do any harm, is not such a good idea.

I hope that after reading this book, you will not see the existing wellbeing programmes as an ultimate solution for enhancing wellbeing in your school. Instead, you will cautiously decide whether the programmes available to you in your geographical area are indeed in line with your school's needs. Also consider a series of ongoing interventions that are either evidence-based, evidence-informed, and/or common sense, which may be just as good a way to improve your school community's wellbeing. Regardless of what interventions or programmes you choose, your starting point will always be deciding on a wellbeing framework. You can choose it from the sample frameworks we discussed in this chapter or create your school's community's own wellbeing framework, by choosing the most applicable components of wellbeing. In the next chapter we will delve into some of these components further.

Take-aways for the school's wellbeing strategy

- The most prevalent, contemporary model of mental health is a continuum between mental illness, languishing, moderate health, flourishing.
- Wellbeing programmes and interventions need to cater for the school community at all points of the continuity model.
- All current models are componental, meaning that they consist of various evidence-based components.

- This offers school communities an opportunity to create their own school-relevant wellbeing framework.
- Each component comes with interventions that show an increase of this component's outcomes when it is practiced.
- Interventions can be evidence-based, evidence-informed or common sense.
- It is important to measure the effectiveness of the specific wellbeing framework and associated interventions to see if as a whole they increase students wellbeing.

References

AFH. 2020. 10 keyes to happier living [Online]. Available: https://www.actionforhappiness.org/10-keys-to-happier-living [Accessed 23rd Sep 2020].

Boniwell, I. 2013. Introduction to positive education. In: David, S. A., Boniwell, I. & Conley Ayers, A. (eds.), *The Oxford Handbook of Happiness*. New York: Oxford University Press.

Burke, J. & Minton, S. J. 2016. Re-thinking well-being measures in bullying and cyberbullying research. In: Mcguckin, C. & Corcoran, L. (eds.), *Bullying and Cyberbullying: Prevalence, Psychological Impacts and Intervention Strategies*. New York: Nova.

Davidson, R. J. & Begley, S. 2012. *The Emotional Life of Your Brain*. London: Hodder & Stoughton.

Diener, E. 1984. Subjective well-being. *Psychological Bulletin*, 95, 542–575.

Diener, E. 2010. New well-being measures: Short scales to assess flourishing and positive and negative feelings. *Social Indicators Research*, 97, 143–156.

Diener, E. & Seligman, M. E. P. 2002. Very happy people. *Psychological Science*, 13, 81.

Diener, E., Suh, E. M., Lucas, R. E. & Smith, H. L. 1999. Subjective well-being: Three decades of progress. *Psychological Bulletin*, 125, 276–302.

Disabato, D. J., Goodman, F. R., Kashdan, T. B., Short, J. L. & Jarden, A. 2016. Different types of well-being? A cross-cultural examination of hedonic and eudaimonic well-being. *Psychological Assessment*, 28, 471–482.

GALLUP. 2020. *What we do* [Online]. Available: https://www.gallup.com/home.aspx [Accessed 23rd Sep 2020].

Griebler, U., Rojatz, D., Simovska, V. & Forster, R. 2017. Effects of student participation in school health promotion: A systematic review. *Health Promotion International*, 32, 195–206.

Huppert, F. A. & So, T. T. C. 2013. Flourishing across Europe: Application of a new conceptual framework for defining well-being. *Social Indicators Research*, 110, 837–861.

Huppert, F. A. & Whittington, J. E. 2003. Evidence for the independence of positive and negative well-being: Implications for quality of life assessment. *British Journal of Health Psychology*, 8, 107.

Kern, M. L., Benson, L., Steinberg, E. A. & Steinberg, L. 2016. The EPOCH measure of adolescent well-being. *Psychological Assessment*, 28, 586–597.

Keyes, C. L. M. 2002. The mental health continuum: From languishing to flourishing in life. *Journal of Health and Social Behavior*, 43, 207–222.

Keyes, C. L. M., Shmotkin, D. & Ryff, C. D. 2002. Optimizing well-being: The empirical encounter of two traditions. *Journal of Personality and Social Psychology*, 82, 1007–1022.

Lai, M. K., Leung, C., Kwok, S. Y. C., Hui, A. N. N., Lo, H. H. M., Leung, J. T. Y. & Tam, C. H. L. 2018. A multidimensional PERMA-H positive education model, general satisfaction of school life, and character strengths use in Hong Kong senior primary school students: Confirmatory factor analysis and path analysis using the APASO-II. *Frontiers in Psychology*, 9, 1090.

Lyubomirsky, S., Sheldon, K. M. & Schkade, D. 2005. Pursuing happiness: The architecture of sustainable change. *Review of General Psychology*, 9, 111–131.

Noble, T. & Mcgrath, H. 2015. PROSPER: A new framework for positive education. *Psychology of Wellbeing*, 5, 2.

Parks, A. C. & Biswas-Diener, R. 2013. Positive interventions: Past, present, and future. In: Kashdan, T. B. & Ciarrochi, J. (eds.), *Mindfulness, Acceptance, and Positive Psychology: The Seven Foundations of Well-Being*. Oakland, CA: Context Press/New Harbinger Publications.

Peterson, C. 2006. *A Primer in Positive Psychology*. New York: Oxford University Press.

Rath, T. & Harter, J. 2010. *Wellbeing: The Five Essential Elements*. New York: Gallup Pr.

Ruini, C. & Fava, G. A. 2009. Well-being therapy for anxiety disorder. Part of special issue on: *Positive Psychology in Clinical Practice*, 65, 510–519.

Rusk, R. D., Vella-Brodrick, D. A. & Waters, L. 2018. A complex dynamic systems approach to lasting positive change: The Synergistic Change Model. *The Journal of Positive Psychology*, 13, 406–418.

Ryff, C. D. 1989. Happiness is everything, or is it? Explorations on the meaning of psychological well-being. *Journal of Personality & Social Psychology*, 57, 1069–1081.

Seligman, M. E. P. 2002. *Authentic Happiness: Using the New Positive Psychology to Realize Your Potential for Lasting Fulfillment*. New York: Free Press.

Seligman, M. E. P. 2011. *Flourish: A Visionary New Understanding of Happiness and Well-Being*. New York: Atria.

Seligman, M. E. P. & Csikszentmihalyi, M. 2000. Positive psychology: An introduction. *American Psychologist*, 55, 5–14.

Sin, N. L. & Lyubomirsky, S. 2009. Enhancing well-being and alleviating depressive symptoms with positive psychology interventions: A practice-friendly meta-analysis. Part of special issue on: *Positive Psychology in Clinical Practice*, 65, 467–487.

Smith, R. 2017. Wearing wellbeing. *The Fashion Studies Journal* [Online]. Available: http://www.fashionstudiesjournal.org/4-notes-from-the-field-3/2017/7/29/wearing-wellbeing. [Accessed on 23rd Sep 2020].

Tudor, K. 1996. *Mental Health Promotion: Paradigms and Practice*. East Sussex: Routledge.

Tugade, M. M. & Fredrickson, B. L. 2004. Resilient individuals use positive emotions to bounce back from negative emotional experiences. *Journal of Personality and Social Psychology*, 86, 320–333.

Vaillant, G. E. 2003. *Aging Well: Surprising Guideposts to a Happier Life*. New York: Little, Brown.

Weare, K. & Nind, M. 2011. Mental health promotion and problem prevention in schools: What does the evidence say? *Health Promotion International*, 26, 29–69.

Westerhof, G. & Keyes, C. 2010. Mental illness and mental health: The two continua model across the lifespan. *Journal of Adult Development*, 17, 110–119.

WHO. 2017. *International Classification of Health Interventions (ICHI)*. Available: https://www.who.int/classifications/ichi/en/. [Accessed on 23rd Sep 2020].

Williams, P. 2011. Pathways to positive education at Geelong Grammar School integrating positive psychology and appreciative inquiry. *AI Practitioner*, 13, 8–13.

CHAPTER

Your guide to the essential elements of wellbeing

Frequently applied components

The evidence-based components of wellbeing discussed in this chapter will help you make an informed-decision, as to what elements should be included in your wellbeing framework. Factors, such as your school culture, past school evaluations, inspectorate reports, school strategy, or very importantly, the needs of your community, should be considered when deciding on which elements you choose to include in your school's wellbeing framework.

In addition to this, a list of sample interventions is presented for each component, which can become a basis for creating a series of school-based interventions in your community. The vast majority of them are evidence-based, a few are evidence-informed. These interventions can be modified to make them age-appropriate and relevant to your specific school-culture and community. I recommend that a wellbeing committee is set up in your school and that both components and interventions featured in this chapter are discussed. We shall start with an all-encompassing component, which is *emotions* that significantly affect all aspects of our daily lives.

Cornucopia of emotions

I have recently visited a *Nurture room* in a primary school for disadvantaged children in Ireland. The two teachers who looked after the children told me stories of young people who came to school frustrated and not knowing how to express their emotions. Over the years, the teachers taught them the language of emotions allowing emotionally illiterate children to walk into the room and tell them: *Today, I feel angry because my dad gave out to me on the way to school*. This ability to recognise emotions is seen as one of the core pathways to mental health. Neuroscientific research indicates that the mere labelling of emotions reduces our emotional reactivity (Lieberman et al., 2007), allowing us to deal more effectively with both our inner and the outside worlds.

With maturity, our emotions become more complex (Fredrickson, 2013), allowing us to experience a cornucopia of emotions which can be beneficial to our health

(Larsen et al., 2003). After all, learning from *the ups and downs of our lives* and an ability to *take the good with the bad* is an ultimate ability we develop that prevents us from suppressing our emotions and ill-health (Hershfield et al., 2013). Emotional suppression is a disadvantage to us, as it is associated with a higher levels of symptoms of psychopathology in childhood and adolescents, such as depression, trauma, anxiety, obsessive-compulsive disorder and others (Compas et al., 2017). Helping young people label and express emotions in an effective way is beneficial for their development and acts as a protective mechanism against acquiring pathologies.

The rapidly developing brains of babies and very young children make them experience a lot of dichotomous emotions (Medina, 2014). When they are sad, they cry, when they are picked up and cuddled by a carer, they stop crying and are content again. As children grow, their emotional system changes and they start to experience a mixture of anger and pride when they defend a bully, or sadness and joy when they reminiscent about their adventures with a grandparent who has recently passed away. However, sometimes despite experiencing the mixture of emotions inside them, they are unable to pinpoint them, because the predominant feelings of anger or sadness take over. Helping young people find names for the cornucopia of emotions they are flooded with can help them cope with life adversities much more effectively. Thus, emotions are often a fundamental part of any wellbeing programme or an intervention.

There are some differences found between genders in the way they deal with emotions. It is not surprising given that we tend to bring up boys and girls differently. Due to the work of the gender equality movement, less people claim that boys should not cry and that girls are more emotional. However, growing research on the topic is showing us some curious results. In a meta-analysis, including 212 studies with over 20, 000 children and young people, the researchers found that the expression of emotions changes for both genders during their childhood (Chaplin and Aldao, 2013). Overall, girls show more internalising emotions, such as sadness or anxiety, whereas boys show more externalising emotions, such as anger. However, there are also some intricacies observed, such as girls showing more positive emotions than boys in their middle childhood and adolescence; boys showing more externalising emotions at toddler/preschool age and middle childhood, and fewer externalising emotions in adolescence. Therefore, somehow, boys become less expressive, as they reach their secondary school.

Emotional Intelligence

We cannot discuss emotions without briefly mentioning Emotional Intelligence (EI), as it is a fundamental wellbeing tool that can be relatively easy to learn. There are at least 10 models of EI. Each one of them conceptualises it differently. One of the most comprehensive definitions states that EI is an ability to recognise own and others' emotions and use them to guide thinking and behaviour (Salovey and Mayer, 1990). Therefore, emotionally intelligent people are able to accurately recognise when they are angry, happy, sad, frustrated, or when they have a mixture of emotions. They are also aware of other people's emotional state by watching their facial expression, behaviour or assessing a situation they find themselves in. More importantly, however, they are able to predict people's behaviours based on other people's emotions, which is useful in preventing conflicts and misunderstandings. They also let their own emotions guide them on how to think and behave in various circumstances. EI is therefore, an essential, high-level processing experience for all.

The current models of EI can be broadly divided into two types: ability models and/or trait models. The trait models view EI as a stable characteristic, a predisposition for emotional awareness and acting in accordance with emotions (Schutte et al., 1998). The ability models see it as a skill that can be developed (Mayer et al., 2003). As a result of viewing EI as an ability, a series of interventions and programmes have been created that help children as young as infants to recognise emotions and act upon them in an appropriate manner. A review of 20 of such educational programmes found that EI interventions were effective across all young people's ages; however, the highest level of effectiveness was reported in younger children (Puertas-Molero et al., 2020). A similar analysis of 58 studies found that EI can also be very effective with adults (Mattingly and Kraiger, 2019). Therefore, an intervention or a programme that taps into the four aspects of EI would be very beneficial to most, if not all young people.

There are many reasons why it is useful to develop these skills. Students with high levels of EI achieve better grades and greater achievement test scores (MacCann et al., 2020). They can manage stress, anxiety and depression more effectively (Resurrección et al., 2014). EI is also associated with higher levels of physical (Martins et al., 2010) and mental (Sánchez-Álvarez et al., 2016) health. Emotionally intelligent teachers are less likely to experience burnout and feel emotionally exhausted after work (Martínez-Monteagudo et al., 2019). Educational leaders with high levels of EI have a better quality interaction with their team, thus practice more effective leadership (Barbuto Jr and Bugenhagen, 2009). These are just a few of the EI list of benefits making it a strong contender for being included in a school's wellbeing strategy, especially given that it is relatively easy for most to learn the language and the meaning of emotions.

Interventions

There are a multitude of socio-emotional interventions for children, adolescents and teachers, the objective of which is to improve EI. Given the interest of young people in gaming, games such as "Spock" may be used to help them identify emotions in self and others, as well as use them appropriately (Cejudo et al., 2019). For younger children, the "Inside out" movie about emotions can be used to discuss what they are and how well they serve us (Benarous and Munch, 2016). In order to understand what emotions we feel, simple naming of emotions when discussing a book character or a situation in school can help students become more aware of what each emotion feels like and what it means. For children, adolescents and adults, some of the exercises that help them manage their emotions effectively include creating a list (older children) or a drawing (younger children) of things they like doing when they feel emotions such as sadness, anger, disappointment. Then, when experiencing negative emotions, we can go to that list/drawings and find tips on what we can do to turn our mood around (McGrath and Noble, 2017).

Positive emotions

For many years, researchers undermined the importance of positive emotions in our lives. In one of the main theories of emotions, Paul Ekman (2004) identified six core emotions based on our facial expression, as fear, anger, disgust, sadness, happiness and surprise, most of which were negative. Negative emotions were seen to serve an important evolutionary purpose of warning us against danger. Positive emotions, on the other hand, were seen as almost unworthy of an empirical inquiry, as they didn't seem to add much to our lives apart from making us happy. All this changed when researchers, such as Alice Isen from Cornell University, demonstrated through a series of experiments that the experiences of positive emotions serve an important purpose in our lives (Moskowitz et al., 2014). She showed us that they facilitate creativity, problem-solving, decision-making and negotiation. Her studies were the basis for the Broaden-and-build theory, according to which positive emotions broaden our minds and build psychological, intellectual and social resources that allow us to thrive (Fredrickson, 2001).

Broaden-and-build is now the main theory about the role that positive emotions play in our psyche. When we help students create positive emotions (Fredrickson and Joiner, 2018), they experience a momentary expansion of ideas, which allows them to come up with more creative solutions to their problems and see perspectives they had never thought existed. When we build a habit of inducing and regularly experiencing positive emotions, they serve us as shields that protect us against pathologies. Finally, positive emotions create a transformative upward spiral that allows us to continue to grow them in the future. Therefore, for students who have experienced a greater frequency of positive emotions pre-crisis, instead of reducing the crisis has amplified their positivity, rather than reducing it, with emotions such as *hope* significantly contributing to the growth of their resilience and wellbeing (Fredrickson et al., 2003). Similarly, during the pandemic, young people were flooded with compassion, sympathy and other positive emotions, instead of experiencing a lot of negativity (Kim and Niederdeppe, 2013), which has helped them cope more effectively in the face of adversity. These are some of the reasons why helping students tap into their positive emotions and develop them further is very useful.

Even though positive emotions are fleeting, when we are able to "catch" them and experience them fully, they help us initiate an avalanche of processes that enhance our long-term wellbeing (Fredrickson and Joiner, 2002). They boost our physical health (Kok et al., 2013), reduce our symptoms of illness, increase our life purpose, and prompt us to seek social support instead of isolating ourselves (Fredrickson et al., 2008). Most importantly, however, they contribute significantly to developing our psychological flourishing (Kahneman et al., 2004) and are useful in turning the vicious cycle of negative emotions into a helpful cycle that reduces suicidal thoughts (Joiner, 2005), depression, anxiety (Garland et al., 2010) and self-harm (Morris et al., 2014). Therefore, positive emotions are not only there to keep us happy, but despite their fleeting nature, they also protect us from experiencing ill-being.

The powerful impact of positive emotions has been practiced in therapy for a long time. Cognitive Behaviour Therapy (CBT) is one of the most prominent therapies worldwide. One of its fundamental ideas is that emotions are connected to our thoughts, physical feelings and behaviour (Beck, 2011). When one of the four elements changes, it has a knock-on effect on others. For many people, one of the easiest elements to alter is emotions. When they are feeling low, they look at a picture of their loved one or put on upbeat music, which may help them temporarily enhance positive emotions. Experiencing more positive emotions acts like a chain reaction affecting our thoughts, body and subsequent behaviour. Once we learn the skill to self-induce more positive emotions, instead of waning, they keep multiplying over time making us feel better about our lives (Moskowitz et al., 2017), helping us change our lifestyle to a more positive one (Van Cappellen et al., 2018). This is why learning to control our emotions more and induce positive emotions when required has a powerful effect not only on wellbeing but also our entire life.

The consequences of not experiencing many positive emotions, especially when facing adversity, are dire. The unfortunate thing is that when going through bad times, our positive emotions are less intense and last a shorter period of time than negative emotions. This means that is it harder to elicit them and make them last. Yet, people who are resilient are more likely to evoke positive emotions through the use of humour, relaxation, optimistic thinking and other effective coping strategies, which helps them bounce back more effectively from adversities (Tugade and Fredrickson, 2004). An inability to elicit such emotions, especially in stressful times, leads to a slower and less efficacious process of adjustment. This is why teaching children and young people how to do it may be beneficial to them for years to come.

Over the last couple of decades, there was an explosion of emotion-related research. This allowed researchers to expand the list of positive emotions. Every year we have thousands of new pieces of research carried out that help us understand the deeper meaning of each positive emotion, intricacies about their conceptualisation or ways in which we can use them to help us live a better life. Table 3.1 lists some of these emotions as per two authorities in this field.

Many wellbeing programmes and interventions in schools work either explicitly or implicitly on enhancing positive emotions, as increase in such emotions lifts students' mood, opens up their minds, allows them to tap into their resources and is simply a fun thing to do. This is why learning about recognising and self-eliciting positive emotions should be a part of the wellbeing strategy in every school.

Interventions
There are plenty of interventions, the aim of which is to enhance positive emotions. One of them is writing about *Intensely Positive Experience* (Burton and King, 2004). Students spent 20 min a day, over three consecutive days, writing about their intensely positive experience. Three months later, they experienced a significant improvement in positive mood and reported fewer visits to a doctor compared with a control group. This is a great activity for boosting positive emotions. Below are a few examples of emotions that students, teachers and parents may find useful and easy to elicit.

TABLE 3.1 A list of positive emotions, adapted from Fredrickson, 2009, and Watson et al., 1988

Active	Enthusiasm	Love
Alert	Gratitude	Pride
Amusement	Inspiration	Relief
Attentive	Interest	Satisfaction
Awe	Joy	Serenity
Determination	Hope	Strength
Excitement		

Gratitude

Gratitude refers to a feeling of appreciation and thankfulness for what we have, or what someone else has done for us. It is both a disposition and a life orientation towards becoming aware and appreciating all that is good in life (Wood et al., 2010). According to some research, boys benefit more from gratitude than girls (Froh et al., 2009). It occurs naturally in adults, but is not as common in children unless prompted by carers, for example, asking young people to say *thank you* after they were given something (Greif and Gleason, 1980). This is why it is crucial to teach children gratitude from early years.

The benefits of gratitude include an improvement in life satisfaction (Emmons and McCullough, 2003), reduction in worry and insomnia, making it a particularly good intervention during the exams (Digdon and Koble, 2011). It helps with creation and maintenance of relationships, which is useful at any time (Algoe et al., 2008). It is particularly useful for students who are experiencing challenges at home and for whom gratitude towards their teachers or other people in their lives helps them cope more effectively with their home-life stressors (Liauw et al., 2018). Systematic gratitude development is also great at protecting us against rumination (dwelling on and playing back some of our negative thoughts and situations) and loneliness (Layous et al., 2014). These are just a handful of the gratitude benefits, and the list goes on and on as it is one of the best researched positive emotions.

When delivering a depression-prevention workshop in a secondary school, a boy I was teaching asked me a challenging question: *If a person has depression, one of the reasons for it is that they are blind to the positive aspects of their lives, and if so, how can they practice gratitude?* I loved the question and enjoyed the challenge. However, contrary to what we might assume about people experiencing depression, research shows us that they can benefit more from it than those who are mentally healthy (Seligman et al., 2006). This may be due to that lower threshold of positivity they experience, allowing just a small effect to be amplified. Gratitude activity was also used with people who were dissatisfied with their body and worry too much (Geraghty et al., 2010). Both studies showed great benefits of practicing gratitude.

Expressing gratitude for teachers is also effective, as it enhances team's creativity (Pillay et al., 2020), which can be particularly useful when redesigning our lesson plans or thinking of novel ideas of how to improve our schools' wellbeing. Also, encouraging teachers to practice gratitude impacts positively on their classroom management and the improvement of the school environment (Howells, 2014). Among school leaders, while expressing daily gratitude was a little frustrating, it resulted in a more balanced perspective on the events occurring in the school (Waters and Stokes, 2015). It also allowed leaders to experience more hopefulness, optimism and happiness, as well as engage in appreciative problem-solving. Overall, it had a very positive effect on leaders and their schools.

Interventions

Gratitude is one of the best-researched interventions. It can be practiced by listing three or five or unlimited things we are grateful for, and we can do it at various frequencies, daily, a few times a week or weekly (Emmons and McCullough, 2003). Please note that too frequent engagement with this activity may cause boredom; therefore, just to get students into a habit of doing it, you may encourage a daily gratitude for 2 weeks or so, but afterwards let them decide how often they wish to do it themselves. Some students may experience an amplification of positive emotions when they not only list what they are grateful for, but also explain the reasons why they are grateful for them (Seligman et al., 2006). Gratitude activity may also be done by looking far back into the past, for example, thinking of the last summer and the things we did for which we are grateful (Watkins et al., 2003). One of the most effective ways in which gratitude is practiced among youth is by asking them to write a *Gratitude Letter* to someone whom they are grateful and deliver it to them personally (Froh et al., 2009). It is shown to significantly boost their positive emotions, and the effect lingers with them for longer.

Gratitude is easy to introduce at the beginning or the end of the class. I remember hearing about a teacher who created a *Gratitude Jar* and each day, on the way home, she asked students to think about *What Went Well* (www) that day, write it down on a piece of paper and drop it into the gratitude jar. Some students apparently loved this activity, as it was a closure to the school day and a harbinger to the post-school fun. I have also heard from many leaders who have introduced "what went well over the last week" activity at the beginning of their meetings and talked about the transformative effect this simple exercise had on the team and how it launched their positive mood trajectory. This culture of gratitude can be easily implemented in any organisation. Therefore, gratitude is great for the entire school community.

Forgiveness

Whenever I lecture students about forgiveness, I see either serenity spreading all over their faces or utter irritation. It amuses me how predictable their reaction is year-on-year. The reason for it is that there are many misconceptions about forgiveness, and until we understand it well, we may judge it incorrectly, and it will be hard for us to decide if we want to forgive or not. In this section, we will look at forgiveness towards others rather than self-forgiveness.

Forgiveness is not about condoning someone's behaviour, justifying them in any way or excusing what they have done. It is about us and how *we* cope in a post-conflict or post-trauma situation. There are two perspectives on forgiveness: (1) decisional and (2) emotional (Worthington, 2006). The decisional type of forgiveness is the choice we make not to retaliate for doing the things that culprits have done. It is a choice we make not to act out of revenge, and instead behave in a pro-social manner towards the perpetrator, while at the same time protecting ourselves from any further hurt they may cause. The second type of forgiveness is emotional, which goes considerably deeper than just making a decision, therefore has more wellbeing benefits associated with it. Emotional forgiveness means that we are able to turn our emotions and thoughts associated with the transgression from negative to positive. This way, when we think about the person who did us wrong, we are no longer flooded with negativity, shame, regret, anger, instead we experience either neutral or positive emotions such as compassion, hopefulness, kindness, hence the serenity on some of my students' faces. Emotional forgiveness is, therefore, about us feeling better and has little to do with the perpetrator. We are the ones forgiving, and we are the ones receiving the benefits of it. The perpetrator is out of the equation.

Lack of forgiveness may cause us harm, as it is associated with higher levels of depression (Myung-Sun, 2016). It may take us sometime to forgive (Worthington et al., 2000); however, when we do it, we no longer feel rejected by others and are able to look at the situation from a less hurtful perspective (Ascioglu Onal and Yalcin, 2017). It also has a positive effect on our wellbeing (Bono et al., 2008), and that effect is significant across various studies (Akhtar and Barlow, 2018), which is enough of a reason to start practicing it. After forgiving someone, our physical health is also improved, as we experience lower levels of stress, heart rate and blood pressure (Vanoyen et al., 2001), decreased anxiety and anger (Subkoviak et al., 1995), since we have left all the bad memories behind. Forgiveness is particularly useful in bullying situations as it reduces the incidents of bullying in school (Ahmed and Braithwaite, 2006).

Teachers see forgiveness differently and mainly from the decisional, and social-issue perspective, in that forgiveness for teachers is a social expectation in a conflict situation in schools (Northern and Lins-Dyer, 2003). When children are fighting, the teachers expect them to forgive each other and move on, which indicates the decisional nature of forgiveness. At the same time, they do not feel the same way about forgiving or pardoning institutions, such as the department/ministry of education or schools, as they do not view it as an attempt to resolve a social issue.

In a classroom situation, both teachers and students can practice forgiveness by giving others yet another chance, letting go, responding with kindness to a tricky school situation and by speaking positively about their perpetrators (Haslip et al., 2019). However, for forgiveness to happen, it cannot be based just on words, decisions and behaviours, but needs to involve the inner peace associated with the past event. This includes a more compassionate view of those who did us wrong.

When youth at risk were asked about forgiveness, half of them did not endorse it and found it difficult to apply it in an interpersonal conflict (Edgar-Smith and Palmer, 2017). However, at the same time, many of them did not know what forgiveness was. This offers an opportunity for schools to teach children about what it is like to forgive, as it may have a more positive effect on their overall lives. Also, it is important to remember that creating a climate of apology and forgiveness is a multilevel process which includes the impact of cultural attitudes towards forgiveness, organisational values, organisational practices and leaders' behaviour (Fehr and Gelfand, 2012). This is why to teach children forgiveness, the school community needs to practice forgiveness too and do it at all levels. Creating such a climate, while time-consuming, may benefit the entire school community and result in enhanced levels of wellbeing. This is a valuable intervention to include in your school's wellbeing strategy.

Interventions

One of the most prominent models of forgiveness is *REACH* (Worthington, 2013). This is an acronym that stands for R – recall the offence that caused us anger, E – practice empathy for the individual or group that offended us, A – commit to altruistically forgive the perpetrators, C – commit to forgiving them and H – hold on to that commitment, as it takes time to forgive. Individuals are asked to move along each step to reach forgiveness. A simple yet powerful intervention that is sometimes used to practice forgiveness is writing a *Letter of Forgiveness* to someone who did us wrong (Lyubomirsky, 2007). However, please note that this exercise may backfire, as it implies students' innocence, whereas many who are practicing it may experience a mixture of guilt and anger (Peterson and Park, 2004), as they believe they may have somewhat contributed to the situation. This is where not only forgiveness towards others but also forgiveness towards self is important.

A special forgiveness curriculum was developed for secondary school students, which allows them to work through four phases of forgiveness: (1) uncovering, (2) decision, (3) work and (4) outcome/deepening (Lin et al., 2013). The first stage involved discussing emotions and talking about feelings associated with the perpetrator and a situation. The second stage was about psychoeducation, learning about what forgiveness actually means and that it is an alternative to retribution. The third stage related to discussing pros and cons about forgiveness so that students could decide if they wanted to practice forgiveness. The final stage was a commitment to forgive. Considering that this process is deep and may uncover a lot of issues, it is recommended that a mental health professional takes students through it. However, in the meantime, parts of it, such as a discussion about what it means to forgive, may become aspects of the wellbeing strategy in school.

The following are three interventions associated with forgiveness that may also be introduced to the school community. The first one is *Emotional Storytelling,* whereby we are asked to tell/write/draw stories about our stressful events and the emotions they elicited in us to allow us to process the events in a healthy way (Greenberge, 2008). The second activity is *Letting Go of Grudges* (Reivich, 2004). In this activity, students are asked to recall a person that they hold a grudge against and write down as many things as they can think of for which they are grateful, in relation to the person or the circumstances. The third one is a *Benefit Finding* intervention (King and Miner, 2000), which is also shown to facilitate forgiveness (McCullough et al., 2006). Students are asked to write an essay or express themselves in other ways, about a hurtful thing that someone did to them, however, they need to do it by recalling positive aspects of this experience. What were the positive consequences of the event? What personal benefits came out of it? Will there be any positive benefits coming out of it in the future? These activities can be also used for entire school community.

Negative emotions

While positive emotions form an important part of the wellbeing programmes, it is crucial not to dismiss our negative emotions. Emotions, regardless of whether they are positive or negative, need to be recognised and acknowledged. When that happens, a healing process may begin.

The sad thing is that negative emotions in others make us often uncomfortable. In a classroom, when a child expresses anger, it is seen as being disrespectful to the teacher and sometimes the young person is scolded for showing this emotion. Also, when we see a student sad, we tell them to cheer up, after all life is too short for a long face. Sometimes, noticing our own or other people's negative emotions makes us feel uncomfortable and to get rid of this feeling as quickly as possible we may try to crush them or disregard them before actually processing them.

Bereavement is one of the most challenging times for anyone, especially a young person, who may have never experienced death of someone close to them. For years, we did not mention the elephant in the room, and in some schools we continue to ignore the loss that children have experienced. Yet, when bereaved children participate in a programme such as a 10-week *Kids Supporting Kids* curriculum, it allows primary school pupils process the death of someone close to them and cope with the bereavement more effectively (Tillman and Prazak, 2018). Children prior to attending the programme said they felt sad that no one was listening to them. This programme made them feel like they were not alone and were able to process their negative feelings and reported experiencing positive emotions as well. This is why helping children not to be scared about their negative emotions, and to learn ways to process them effectively, may be part of the wellbeing strategy.

Interventions

One of the most powerful activities that helps us cope more effectively with negative thoughts and emotions is *Expressive Writing*, which is encouraging students to sit down for 20 min every day for a number of days and write about their deepest thoughts and feelings associated with a specific event that caused them upset (Pennebaker, 1997). It is used extensively in therapy and as part of some wellbeing programmes (Pennebaker, 2018). It is very helpful to adolescents, especially those with high levels of emotional problems who have seen the most significant improvements in their wellbeing after carrying out this intervention (Travagin et al., 2015), children with learning disabilities (Gersten and Baker, 2001) and it can be interwoven into curriculum, such as expressive writing in the science class (Dorroh, 1993). It helps us improve our mood, cope more effectively with episodes of anxiety (Pennebaker, 2018) and is also beneficial for people with depression; however, the effect of it is not long lasting, unless they are involved in the activity frequently over a longer period of time (Reinhold et al., 2018). Handwriting seems to provide more benefits than typing (Brewin and Lennard, 1999), and students should be encouraged to go deeper into their thoughts, as thoughtful writing showed more powerful effects (Pennebaker, 2018). Whenever I suggest this activity to anyone, I always reassure them that the writing they do is for their eyes only and should be disposed of as soon as they finish it to prevent them from unnecessary re-living their negative experiences. Finally, for any bilingual students, it is recommended that writing is done in both languages, as thoughts might flow easily without the language barriers (Kim, 2008). It is a great activity to use for teachers and school leaders, especially after a challenging day at school.

Another example of how to deal with negative emotions is by engaging in self-compassion. Self-compassion is a process of "being open to and moved by one's own suffering, experiencing feelings of caring and kindness towards oneself, taking an understanding, non-judgemental attitude towards one's inadequacies and failures, and recognising that one's experience is part of the common human experience" (Neff, 2003). When we are experiencing negative events in our lives, self-compassion can protect us against negative emotions directed at self (Leary et al., 2007). It is particularly effective when we feel shameful about something. For example, if we receive ambivalent feedback about our performance and tend to beat ourselves up over it, the healing power of self-compassion can help us bounce back and turn the negative emotions into positive. Teachers who have learnt self-compassion through mindfulness were left with a stronger feeling that they are capable teachers and it reduced their feelings of shame (Akpan and Saunders, 2017). For adolescents who are ashamed of their bodies, self-compassion prevents them from sustaining a distorted body image (Wang et al., 2020). For those who are anxious and experience mood and anxiety disorder, self-compassion reduces their symptoms (Finlay-Jones,

2017). In general, developing self-compassion is effective in preventing adolescent depression, a symptom of which is experiencing a higher level of negative emotions (Pullmer et al., 2019).

Here are three activities associated with self-compassion (Neff, 2020). In the first activity *How Would You Treat a Friend?* we are asked to reflect on how we treat our friends when they struggle and then think about how we treat ourselves when we struggle. Can we tell any differences between these two situations? If so, we need to write down what changes we would like to make in our treatment of self so that we respond to our struggle in the same way as we would respond to our friend's struggle. The second activity is called a *Compassion Break*. We are asked to recall some stressful time and say to ourselves and embody our words (1) This is a moment of suffering, for example, ouch, it hurts; (2) Suffering is part of life, for example, that's common humanity, I'm not alone, other people feel the same way; (3) Kindness to self, for example, how can I express kindness to myself right now? This activity is based on a recollection of a stressful, hurtful event, but it can also be done while we are in the middle of a stressful time. The third activity is called *Changing Your Critical Self-talk*. Neff (2020) suggests we do it regularly over several weeks as only then it may have a lasting effect on our relationship with ourselves. We can do this exercise either by writing down our thoughts or via internal dialogue. That said, other researchers found that writing and talking to others about defeats was more effective in improving their wellbeing than thinking about them (Lyubomirsky et al., 2006); therefore, this exercise may be more effective if done in writing. Step 1 is to notice when we are being self-critical, the situations in which we do it, the way we go about it (the tone of our voice, frequency, etc) and the words we use. We can do it in real time or by recalling several past situations. In step 2, we make an effort to soften the language we use about ourselves, for example, instead of saying: *You disgust me!*, we soften it by saying: *I don't like what you do*. In Step 3, we reframe what we have done that disgusted us so much, in other words, we explain the reasons as to why we may have done something and do it in a supportive way. The author suggests that we can even stroke or touch our arm, as if we were comforting ourselves and say things like: *Honey, I know it is difficult for you right now, and this is why you didn't study for this test. You just don't have the headspace to do it with everything that is going on in your life*. The focus of this section was self-compassion, but practicing compassion towards others for 10–15 min a day is also beneficial to us and can enhance our happiness and self-esteem (Mongrain et al., 2011).

Hope

There are plenty of books about hope, and there is a reason for this. Hope is a concept that helps us survive and keeps us well, even in the most desperate circumstances. There are at least 30 theories and/or definitions of hope, and two main perspectives on it. The first one considers hope as an emotion; therefore, hope is a feeling of positive anticipation about the future, and the second perspective sees it as cognition – a thinking process that results in a feeling of hope. In the vast literature about hope, the cognitive view is a predominant perspective.

Whether or not we have it, hope depends largely on our environment, such as school or our home, as well as the goals we set up for ourselves (Averill et al., 1990). Hope is most effective when our goals are important to us, when they follow social and moral guidelines, when we feel they are attainable and we have a level of control over them. In these circumstances our hope towards reaching our goals increases.

The most prevalent model of hope considers it as goal-directed thinking that is both motivating and allows us to come up with routes for achieving goals (Snyder et al., 2003). It is about having the will (agency) and coming up with the way (pathways) to accomplish what we are hoping for. This model was introduced in schools all over the US as a *Making Hope Happen* programme (Lopez, 2013b). Its premise was to teach students what hope is all about and construct new beliefs and skills that allow them stay highly motivated and come up with a plan on how to get what they are hoping for. However, some researchers have questioned the model by saying that it does not explain why some people are hopeful despite having nothing to look forward to (Tong et al., 2010). For these people hope might not necessarily be a pragmatic thinking process, but a belief or a feeling that we can achieve something even though we currently can't think of ways to do it.

Hope is particularly important for young people as it determines positive youth development and is associated with life satisfaction (Marques et al., 2013), self-worth, better school attendance, higher grades, physical health and overall wellbeing (Snyder et al., 2018). Students who are hopeful look forward to their future, are fully engaged at school and are less likely to skip classes (Lopez, 2013a). When we face adversity, practicing hope is one of the most useful coping strategies (Lazarus, 1999). It is beneficial in situations, such as transition from one school to another, as it allows students to set up a pathway and create an agency to make it happen (Akos and Kurz, 2016). When life is becoming difficult or at least not satisfactory, having hope allows us to look beyond the today into a brighter future.

Interventions

The good news is that students who experience the least amount of hope benefit from interventions the most (Marques et al., 2014). One of the activities we can guide them through to enhance hope is by helping them set up goals relating to all aspects of their lives, prioritise them well and track their goal progress (Snyder et al., 2003). The most effective goals have specific characteristics (Lyubomirsky, 2007). They are intrinsic, meaning that we want to do them ourselves, rather than because we are influenced by someone. Goals need to be self-concordant, meaning that they are congruent with our own values. Approach-oriented goals are more effective than avoidance goals. Therefore, it is better to say: *I want to increase my optimism,* rather than *decrease pessimism*. They should be harmonious with each other, in that one goal does not stand in the way of reaching another goal. We need to be flexible in the way we approach them. When necessary, we may slightly change them if they prove inappropriate for us. That flexibility allows us to adapt to new circumstances more effectively. Helpful goals are also broken down into manageable chunks, so that we know what goal we need to achieve this week to contribute to the bigger goal next year.

For younger children, hope interventions included picking out pictures of hope, which they then discuss with their peers (Lopez, 2013a), daydreaming of the future, drawing rainbows and flowers as symbols of hope and discussing what hope means to children (McGrath and Noble, 2017). *The Building Hope for the Future* programme is yet another whole-school approach (parents and teachers) for boosting hope, which incorporates the hope theory mentioned earlier and guides students through the practice of clear goal setting, finding out ways to achieve goals, rephrasing any obstacles that students may be facing and giving tips on how to maintain motivation for goal setting (Marques et al., 2011).

Two effective methods in education for dealing with obstacles to a goal achievement are the *Implementation Intention* and *Mental Contrasting* (Hauser, 2018). The implementation intension refers to a situation when we plan what we will do with an obstacle when/if it occurs. For example, *I need to study for my test. I will switch off my phone, so that nobody interrupts me.* The second method is mental contrasting, which means that every time we are tempted by something, we contrast our ideal outcomes with the consequences of indulging in our urges. Therefore, *I need to study for my test. When I feel like doing something else, I imagine failing my test and not doing well for the whole year.* Contrasting my actions today with the worst-case scenario can motivate me to work. Both methods were effective when applied in general, as well as in special education.

In relation to hope as an emotion, a great activity that can enhance it is a *Best Possible Self* intervention (King, 2001). Whereas the previous interventions were focussed on creating specific goals and pathways on how to achieve it, this activity allows us to dream. Students are asked to sit down, think about their lives in the future and imagine that everything has gone as well as it possibly could and all their dreams have been realised. Then, they are asked to write about it for 20 minutes. Alternatively, they can draw it or share their dreams with their friends. For a community-intervention, you may create a project whereby the entire community will come up with the *Best Possible School* ideas.

Engagement

"*If you are bored, go and do something with yourself*" I used to hear my nana, who was always too busy to sit down, say. When she was a child, she looked after her family and in her spare time, she drew portraits and landscapes. During her early adulthood she fought as an underground soldier in WW2. When the war was over, she got married and her six offsprings kept her busy. Later on in life, after she retired, she kept herself occupied by joining various clubs, a church choir and organising charity events. I have lived my life watching my nana fully engaged with all she was doing, always convinced that boredom, or lack thereof, is a choice. This is why it came to me as a surprise when I came across a study that saw boredom as a character trait.

The state of boredom is "the actual experience of boredom in a given moment," as opposed to the trait boredom, which is "an individual's propensity or disposition towards becoming bored" (Fahlman et al., 2013). When we have a predisposition to being bored, it is considerably harder for us to be engaged. Boredom occurs due to the individual's lack of engagement, which is the fundamental prerequisite for motivation. Motivation, on the other hand, is required for individuals to reduce boredom in their lives. This is why academically bored students usually don't fare well in their exams and assessments, as they lack the motivation to go deeper into the topic, resulting in shallow knowledge and lower grades (Hemmings et al., 2019). Since engagement is the first step towards banishing boredom, it is important to identify what it actually means, what is the effect of engagement on wellbeing and how we can increase our engagement within various aspects of our lives.

A couple of decades ago, in ground-breaking research, over 100 highly creative individuals who affected popular culture, such as famous ballerinas, artists, politicians and others were observed, interviewed, analysed, and the researcher found that one thing that all of them had in common was the frequent experiences of flow (Csikszentmihalyi, 1997). Flow is characterised as a state an absolute concentration or absorption in an activity, which can be either physical (e.g., dancers, joggers) or mental (e.g., solving a puzzle) that results in an individual functioning at their fullest capacity. In practical terms, it is a state of losing ourselves in an activity to an extent where we don't know where we are, who we are with or lose tract of time, because all we are focussed on is the activity at hand. While in the middle of experiencing flow, we are unaware of it, because as soon as the awareness emerges, the flow experience subsides, and only then, after being in flow for a while, we are flooded with positive emotions.

The challenge with flow is that not everyone is engaged enough to experience it. Approximately, 10–15% of the US and European population reported that they had never experienced the sensation of flow, with only 10–15% experiencing it daily, while for the majority of us, the flow experience is sporadic (Hefferon and Boniwell, 2011). The reason for the disparity in these statistics is twofold. Firstly, some of us have an autotelic personality making us more likely to experience flow. People with autotelic personality are naturally curious and interested in life, persistent, not too self-conscious, have a propensity for experiencing intrinsic motivation, enjoy challenges, are able to turn boredom into interest, control their attention, set up goals, have a willingness to develop their skills, and these are just some of their personal characteristics (Tse et al., 2020a). Those who are lucky to experience frequent flow also have a higher level of self-reported wellbeing (Tse et al., 2020b). Secondly, sometimes the reason for not experiencing flow frequently is because we don't know how to induce it. Therefore, the awareness of flow and ways in which we can create conditions for experiencing it may help us tap into this wonderful state of mind.

In a school situation, flow is a useful technique for enhancing students' success and wellbeing. In adults, the most frequent experiences of wellbeing occur during our leisure time (Isham et al., 2019). When adolescents' daily activities were analysed, it transpired that 60% of their structured leisure activities provided them with the highest levels of flow during the day, compared to studying at home (over 30%) and classwork, which mostly caused them apathy followed by flow (both at over 20%) (Freire, 2004). This is corroborated by another study showing that students spend approximately a third of their time passively attending to their classes (Shernoff et al., 2003). The most effective activities increasing engagement in class were individual and group work. The least flow-inducing activities were a lecture-style delivery, watching TV/video or taking a test. A longitudinal study with adolescents found that when their engagement increased, so did their intrinsic motivation, self-esteem and the time spent doing homework (Hektner and Csikszentmihalyi, 1996). This is a very good reason as to why we should help students find their flow. Even though flow is self-induced, schools can create environments that allow student and teachers to experience flow more frequently (Shernoff, 2012). This also highlights the importance of the pedagogy for wellbeing becoming an integral part of the wellbeing strategy for schools.

Flow is a familiar experience for many teachers (Tardy and Snyder, 2004). When teaching, flow happens in times when we are interested and involved in our topic.

It is not something that we can plan, as it happens spontaneously, but when it does, it offers us some profound moments of learning. Teachers experiencing flow has a very positive effect on students, who pick up on their excitement about the topic and become just as interested in it (Nakamura and Csikszentmihalyi, 2005). When teaching, sometimes we are in sync with students, which is described as "group flow," a new concept that has emerged suggesting that the same level of absorption that can happen at an individual level is also possible at a group level (Pels et al., 2018).

Flow is just one perspective on engagement. At a whole-school level, the parental or family engagement in their children's school activities is of upmost importance to ensure their wellbeing (Reinke et al., 2019). It refers to the active involvement of parents in their children's education, along with a development of quality parent–teacher relationship. Family–school engagement is associated with better teacher–student relationship 6 months later and student's higher level of engagement (Cheung, 2019), as well as improved peer relationships, better classroom concentration and a reduction in their disruptive behaviour (Smith et al., 2019). Family–school involvement in wellbeing interventions is particularly relevant, if we want to ensure that the whole-school–community approach is effective. Yet, when asked about their perceptions of the quality of school's mental health promotion, parents' impression of their own parenting capabilities influenced their views (Askell-Williams, 2016). The lesser their belief that they can parent their children well, the less value they put on the school's wellbeing initiatives, the less engaged they were with the school newsletters, activities and other initiatives, and ironically their children's mental health was lower, in comparison to the children whose parents believed that they were good parents. This means that possibly the families that need these interventions more are less likely to engage with them. Therefore, specific provisions need to be made for them in the school's wellbeing strategy.

Interventions

Certain conditions can help us experience flow more frequently and become more engaged in what we do (Csikszentmihalyi, 2009). Firstly, we are more likely to experience flow when our activities are structured, rather than free flowing. Also, we can find it easier when a challenge matches our skill. This is a significant condition for flow-induction as we may try and create it by challenging ourselves on the usual activities we do, for example, if you like swimming, challenge yourself every day as to the number of lengths of the swimming pool you do or reduce the amount of time it takes you to do 20 lengths. This challenge which stretches our skills without overwhelming us can induce a flow experience. We are more likely to experience flow when we are able to experience full concentration on the task at hand and feel we have control over the outcome; when we have intrinsic motivation to do the task and do it for the sake of it (Csikszentmihalyi, 2009).

Apart from creating conditions that allow us to create flow, there are a couple of activities that can be introduced to students to make them aware of flow and practice it (Shernoff and Anderson, 2014). The first one is an introduction to what flow is and then a large group discussion about it, during which students share their specific experiences of flow. In the second intervention, students are divided into smaller groups and have 30 min or so to design an activity that fosters flow. Then, each group shares their experiences. These activities were part of a long intervention, thus evaluated as part of the programme, not individually. Nonetheless, they may be useful when introducing flow to students. Another evidence-informed intervention is to write down three activities that we did in the past to help us experience flow and over the next week, practice at least one of them, making it part of our daily routine (Boniwell and Tunariu, 2019).

There are many programmes and interventions for engaging families into school-life. For example, a *Wise Feedback Intervention*, the aim of which is to build parent-teacher trust by asking teachers to construct a "wise" letter to parents with feedback about their children (Houri et al., 2019). In the letter, teachers were asked to include three essential details: (1) a positive greeting, (2) stipulating a specific reason for the communication and advising of a desired outcome, (3) a "wise statement" that alluded to teacher's high expectation of the student's ability to meet or exceed them. This is a teacher's belief that the student can do well. The letter resulted in a significant increase of parental engagement with school. Therefore, it may be a beneficial activity for teachers in your school to do.

Strengths

For decades, if not centuries, teachers discussed values with students. Values refer to the individuals' beliefs about what is important to them. To some, being authentic may be the most important value in life. To others, honesty and kindness are the qualities that guide their choices in life. For most of us values remain at an implicit level, whereby we act according to our values without reflecting upon them. Sometimes, our values are more explicit, and we are able to identify what they are, as well as make conscious decisions in life based on our value-system.

Having values and living our values are two different things. We may value something but not take the time to enact our values on a daily basis. On the other hand, we may engage fully in the values we have, and when we do so, our enacted values become our strengths that contribute to our character development. This is why the Values-in-Action (VIA) model is commonly referred to as Character Strengths (Peterson and Seligman, 2004).

In order to use our strengths daily, we need to firstly become aware of them. Strength-awareness is not common among adults, as barely one in three people are able to articulate what their strengths are (Hill, 2001). When I came across this statistic, it astounded me and I began to wonder why strength-identification is such a rarity. One reason I came up with was that perhaps we do not have the lingo necessary to articulate what is important to us and what we are good at. With this in mind, I supervised a project, with participants who were secondary school leavers, about to embark into the big world of either employment or third level education. We provided them with a list of character strengths and a brief definition of each one of them. We asked them to read all strength-descriptions carefully and identify their top five strengths. Afterwards, they completed the VIA strengths inventory, which assessed their top strengths, and we tried to match their own views of what their top strengths were with the views generated by the psychological test. To our surprise, only 7% of young people were able to accurately guess what their top strengths were. It highlighted to us the importance of teaching students' strengths.

In a study with approximately 10,000 people in New Zealand (Hone et al., 2015), those who were aware of their strengths were nine times more likely to flourish psychologically in comparison to those who were unaware of their strengths. Furthermore, those who used their strengths regularly at work were 18 times more likely to flourish psychologically than those who did not. While this study was carried out with adults, I am guessing it would not be much different for young people. Past research shows us that discussing VIA with pupils and teaching them how they can use them in daily situations can enhance their self-esteem, life satisfaction (Freire et al., 2018), wellbeing (Oppenheimer et al., 2014) and facilitate their positive transition from primary to secondary school (Bharara, 2019). Therefore, strengths can act both as protective mechanisms against some challenging situations as well as building blocks for enhanced wellbeing.

In a study carried out with almost 3,000 secondary school children, I asked them to complete a series of assessments measuring whether or not they were targets or perpetrators of either traditional or cyberbullying (Burke and McGuckin, in press). It transpired that all non-targets and non-perpetrators of both types of bullying had one strength in common, which was prudence. Prudence denotes caution, an ability to consider the consequences of our behaviour, and knowing when enough is enough (Peterson and Seligman, 2004). It is one of the least prevalent strengths worldwide (McGrath, 2015) and belongs to a group of phasic strengths that are used only in specific situation, such as bullying, rather than in our daily lives (Niemiec, 2018). Other strengths that some of the students not engaged in bullying also displayed were fairness, love, spirituality and gratitude (Burke and McGuckin, in press). Considering that young people not engaged in traditional and cyberbullying had these specific strengths in common, it may be possible in the future to create interventions that help students develop them as protective factors against school-bullying.

In relation to teachers, the most effective ones, measured by the gains of their students in standardised tests, had three strengths developed to a higher level: (1) social intelligence, (2) zest and (3) humour (Park and Peterson, 2009). Therefore, they were sensitive to the social cues, enthusiastic and able to put smile on students' faces. Moreover, a thing as simple as spotting students' strengths in a classroom increased classroom engagement, even though it did not necessarily enhance teachers' wellbeing (Quinlan et al., 2019). Therefore strength interventions with all their benefits could become an integral part of a school's wellbeing strategy.

Interventions

There are only a small number of evidence-based interventions applied with children in a school situation (Quinlan et al., 2012), which include such activities as asking students to identify and select strengths (either top strengths or their bottom strengths) which they wish to develop. Students may be asked to identify strengths that have impacted on their past and potential future success, or use their five top strengths in a school setting, perhaps when preparing for an important exam or when trying to make friends (Austin, 2005). They may also start recognising strengths in others and building any new strengths they wish to develop (Proctor et al., 2011).

Yet another way to introduce strengths is via a whole-school intervention by story-telling at school gatherings about the strengths of various people and groups in the school community, as well as encouraging the school's community-wide strength-use (Govindji and Linley, 2008). Finally, past research shows that people who loved their jobs (perceived jobs as a calling) used between four and seven strengths at work daily (Harzer and Ruch, 2012). Therefore, a good intervention for teachers is to identify their own strengths by going to www.viacharacter.org and using four of their top strengths more frequently at work every day (Harzer and Ruch, 2016), especially when they are going through difficult times at work.

Relationships

"*Other people matter*" was a famous saying by Christopher Peterson, one of the main researchers in positive psychology, who continued to highlight the importance of relationships in our lives (Peterson, 2013). A need for relatedness is one of our basic needs, and it refers to connecting meaningfully to another person (Ryan and Deci, 2000). In school, children's need for relatedness is either satisfied or they feel frustrated about it. When it is satisfied, they feel like they are part of a group to which they belong. When they are frustrated, they feel isolated and socially excluded. This is why, it may be necessary that any relationship-oriented interventions in school should address students from these two groups differently (Schmidt et al., 2020). Those, who are frustrated may need to change their cognitive framework and deal with some of their self-limiting beliefs about friendships. On the other hand, students who are satisfied may learn ways to maintain their positive relationships that allows them to flourish.

Regardless of our personality, being around other people makes us happy. When individuals' happiness was measured at various points during the day, they were the happiest when in a company of other people, and the least happy when alone (Kahneman et al., 2004). Experiencing so much socially induced happiness may be due to the fact that we are 30 times more likely to laugh when in a group situation than in solitude (Provine, 2000). But there is more to relationships than happiness, because other people offer us their invaluable support when we need it. Our need for it decreases steadily with age (Keyes, 2002), and the size of our network starts to dwindle in our 30s (Burke, 2017), which is why the highest levels of support and guidance we require is during our childhood. In a longitudinal study with children at-risk, those who grew up to live a fulfilling life talked about a relationship they had had with an adult, other than their carer, who was present in their childhood and provided them with support they required (Werner, 1993). Another longitudinal study found that even those who did not have a supportive adult in childhood, found one in adulthood, for example, a wise friend or a spouse that helped them learn more adaptive ways to live a better life (Vaillant, 2003). Friends, therefore, provide us with laughter, life-skills and growth.

Our friendships with peers are a fundamental part of our development, and among children and adolescents, half of their friendships are stable and ongoing for years, regardless of their gender (Meter and Card, 2016). The factors that predict children's relationship stability were the convenience of friends living nearby or attending summer activities together. However, the most important factor for long-term, stable relationships with friends was their school, featuring in almost all research. Similarly, for adults, approx. 30% of adult friendships usually start at work (Hoggard, 2005). This means that the school is a hub for teachers' and students' friendships to develop; a place that helps them belong. Let us now review research about one type of belonging, which is a highly relevant school-belonging.

Isolation is one of the world's most effective tortures (Myers, 1992), and this is how some students feel when they don't belong. In a school-context, a sense of belonging to a school is associated with students feeling supported, accepted and respected (Goodenow, 1993). In order to feel they belong, they need to share the school's values, feel like they can contribute and make a difference to their school community, and ultimately they need to want to belong to the school community as belonging is reciprocal (Maher et al., 2013). This is why, it is of upmost importance to create a school environment and lead it in a way that makes it attractive for the young members of the school community to want to belong.

Teachers have a huge impact on students' sense of belonging. In fact, some researchers claim that teacher support is so fundamental to experiencing belonging that without it, a sense of belonging to school declines (Allen et al., 2017). This support is particularly important when students experience some problems in school. When teachers' relationships with students are based on fairness and genuine care, when in trouble, instead of drifting away, students' sense of belonging to their school increases. They are also less likely to play truant (Demanet and Van Houtte, 2012), report more engagement (Freeman et al., 2007) and the belonging enhances their wellbeing (Lambert et al., 2013, Šeboková et al., 2018). These are just some of the benefits that derive from good relationships between teachers and students.

Given the high levels of emigration, and diverse school environments around the world, the research about a sense of belonging has never been more timely. Most of the literature associated with a sense of belonging to school tackles the importance of inclusion of minority groups. It considers students with special needs, various sexual orientations or third culture kids (TCK), who are children being brought up in a culture different to their parents' backgrounds. There is a growing number of TCK around the world. At home, they live by the norms of one culture, in school by the norms of another, which prompts them to negotiate their own, third culture, which is an amalgamation of the two cultures that are influencing them. Unlike other children, TCK's belonging is not associated with their country of birth or residence. They often feel disconnected to their environment and somewhat rootless (Van Reken and Pollock, 1999). However as adults, most of them mention that one place where they felt they fully belonged, which was their school, as it provided them with an institutional stability. This is why for TCK children, it is particularly important that a sense of belonging is added into the school's wellbeing strategy.

The process of belonging needs to happen as a whole-school approach, rather than a once-off intervention. Especially, given that it is a dynamic, ever-changing process, rather than a static condition. In a survey carried out in Australia, only 50% of schools had developed a policy about school-belonging (Allen et al., 2017). At the same time, having a policy predicted students' highest scores on a questionnaire that measured school-belonging, making it an important component of a wellbeing strategy.

Interventions

Some of the factors that influence school-belonging are (1) the support students receive from parents, teachers and peers; (2) their involvement in extracurricular activities in the school and (3) perceived school safety, which is both physical and psychological (Allen et al., 2018). Therefore, to boost school-belonging, provisions should be made to help students develop positive relationships with others. Also, ensure that students have extracurricular activities organised for them, and that the school environment is pleasant enough so that they want to stay after hours and hang out with their friends. Finally, in relation to the psychological safety, schools need to promote an environment where students are not afraid to make mistakes.

Other strategies that enhance school-belonging and are easy to implement are ensuring that all children, without exception, are provided with academic support and highly capable teachers are recruited who not only teach effectively but also create clear expectations as to what they need students to do (Wingspread, 2004). Also, fair and consistent disciplinary policies are put in place and there are opportunities for parents and families to be involved in their children's school lives. When setting up norms for enhancing connectedness in school, happy teachers were also considered important, which is why another strategy mentioned by the declaration specified that school staff would be offered support and continuous professional development to enhance their wellbeing.

Interventions for enhancing belonging include writing a *Gratitude Journal* (Diebel et al., 2016). In this study, students were asked to write every day for 4 weeks, two or three things they are grateful for in their schools. When compared with pupils who wrote daily about two to three things that happened in school that day, the group that exercised their gratitude had a significantly higher levels of a school-belonging. Another intervention comes from one of my students, Grainne Dunleavy, who designed a four-session workshop in a primary, international school (Dunleavy and Burke, 2019). She drew from the research by Glasser (1999) and asked pupils to create BINGO cards (quality world pictures) that best describe some of their values relating to love and belonging, fun, power and freedom. Then, they went around the room familiarising themselves with other pupils' values and noting the values they shared. Finally, the class finished with a value-bingo game using the cards pupils created. The aim of the activity was to help pupils get to know each other on a deeper level. Any activities that allow students to share their deeper interests and values may enhance their sense of belonging.

A very well-known intervention that aims to improve the quality of our relationships with others is the *Active-Constructive Responding* (Gable et al., 2004). According to this model, there are four ways in which we respond to good news shared with us by our loved ones, friends and colleagues: (1) passive destructive, for example, after hearing good news we changes the subject ignoring what was said; (2) passive constructive, for example, after hearing good news we say: *that's nice* and don't make a big deal out of the news; (3) active destructive, for example, after hearing the good news, we act like kill-joys pointing out to the problems associated with the good news; (4) active constructive, for example, we react to the news with great enthusiasm and interest. Research shows that only the active-constructive reaction to good news helps relationships thrive.

Another, series of interventions come from the research on kindness, which is associated with pro-social, relationship-enhancing behaviour. However, in addition to improving relationships, it also has a positive effect on our wellness. When we feel blue, pop-psychology literature suggests we should go and spoil ourselves. However, research disagrees, showing that self-indulgence does not improve our wellbeing (Nelson et al., 2016). Instead, when feeling low, becoming other-focussed, practicing altruism and performing *Acts of Kindness* boost our happiness and wellbeing

(Curry et al., 2018) and here are some suggestions on how to do it. You may choose to (1) purchase something for someone, for example, buy a bowl of soup for a homeless person or a cup of coffee for the stranger queuing behind you in a coffee shop or buy one of your friends a gift; (2) donate something; (3) practice social recycling, for example, dispose of your used products by giving them to other consumers free of charge and (4) the most popular random or not-so-random (planned) acts of kindness. There are intricacies about the Acts of Kindness, in that they are more beneficial if we perform a few acts of kindness on one day rather than spread them across the week (Lyubomirsky et al., 2005). Finally, another kindness-related activity is a *Gift of Time*, whereby we are giving someone a gift of your time, by volunteering to do something for them weekly (Fredrickson, 2009).

Meaning and Purpose

There are many definitions of meaning in life. For some meaning is an attainment of our personally valued goals (Ryff and Singer, 1998); for others it is the realisation of the order and purpose of our existence (Reker and Wong, 1988). Yet some see it as a life of purpose, a life that matters and a life that makes sense (Heintzelman and King, 2014). The most prevalent definition incorporates a consistency in understanding ourselves, in the context of our life and having a clear life purpose (Steger et al., 2015). Therefore, it is about knowing who we are, why we are here, what is important to us, what we are hoping to achieve and comprehending how our life experiences have shaped us into the people we are today. While *meaning* refers to the theoretical aspect of our experience, *purpose* is the application of it. Also, meaning *in* life is different to the meaning *of* life, which questions our existence.

Understanding our meaning in life is associated with higher levels of physical health (Roepke et al., 2014). It reduces pathologies and enhances many aspects of our wellbeing (Steger, 2017). It also works in reverse, whereby enhancing mood improves our meaning in life (Hicks and King, 2009). Most importantly, however, meaning offers mental health protection during testing times (Wong, 2011), more so than experiencing positive emotions or any other types of wellbeing components. It helps us make sense of our suffering. Please note that while the presence of life meaning is associated with higher levels of wellbeing, *searching* for meaning hallmarks an inverse effect (Li et al., 2020).

Life purpose, on the other hand, is a motivational and practical aspect of meaning in life (Steger, 2012). My meaning in life may be *growth*, and I may try and think of ways in which I can achieve growth in my life, such as by becoming a teacher, so that I can grow and constantly learn with my students every day. Purpose is associated with goals we set up for ourselves. If we have a meaning in life, but no purpose, it is possible that we can't find the strength or courage to pursue what we value the most. If we don't have a meaning, but have a life purpose, we may realise halfway through our lives that what we do and what we value is not congruent with each other. The best match is to know our meaning and purpose, all at the same time.

I recently spoke at a conference for school leaders in the UK and prior to doing my talk, I had asked them to complete a survey. What transpired was that most of the leaders experienced very high levels of stress at work on a daily basis, but the odd thing was that their wellbeing was maintained at moderate or flourishing levels. When I delved deeper into my data, I found the explanation for it. All the participants of the survey scored extremely high on their measures of meaning for work. No matter how many daily hassles they experienced, or how many unpleasant conversations they have had, it all just made sense to them, they knew why they were doing it, so the stress didn't matter as much (even though given a choice, they would have preferred not to be stressed). Curiously, this is not unusual. When teachers were asked why they work with trauma-affected, struggling students, many of them said that the main reason for it was that it gave their work a meaning (Brunzell et al., 2018). Therefore, when the struggle comes, so does the meaning in life. It is there to support us in adversity and give us direction when we can't make sense of things, which is why we need to nurture it daily.

Younger people are in the process of establishing their life meaning, which is why some of them may not yet know what the meaning of their lives is, others may have an indefinite meaning, yet some may be clear about their meaning (García-Alandete et al., 2018). In order to identify what our meaning in life is, we need to be capable of abstract thinking, and the research is inconsistent about the age at which children can do this; in general it ranges from the age of 6 to 11 (Shoshani and Russo-Netzer, 2017). Therefore, interventions about meaning in life can be introduced to primary school children.

Interventions

Mindfulness meditation is effective at improving meaning in life (Chu and Mak, 2019). Therefore, selecting mindfulness sessions suitable to your community may help them improve their meaning in life. Also, given that using strengths at work boosts the presence of our meaning in life (Littman-Ovadia and Steger, 2010), applying character strengths from the previous section may be helpful to enhance this component of wellbeing. The PURE model of meaning-making is about reflecting upon our lives at any stage (Wong, 2011). We start with (P) Purpose is about life goals and needs; continue on to (U) Understanding what life is all about, what is the meaning of life; (R) Responsibility refers to social or moral responsibility and commitment; (E) Enjoyment/evaluation is about experiencing positive emotions by going through this process.

Another activity that helps us realise our meaning in life comes in various forms. In *Positive Legacy*, we are asked to write about how we would like others to remember us (Rashid and Seligman, 2019). Alternatively, a more gloomy version of it is the "*Most Feared Obituary*," where we may pretend that we have failed to change the unhealthy and unhappy ways in which we live our lives and things will get worse as we age (Frisch, 2006). Then, we are encouraged to write our own obituary, just before we die, for our family and friends. I am not a fan of this activity as it sends chills down my spine, but some of my colleagues and friends who did it found it useful. It is also an activity featuring in the Quality of Life therapy.

Accomplishment

When working with adults with depression, helping them experience a sense of accomplishment was one of my objectives. This sense of accomplishment came from simple tasks, such as tidying up their kitchen, calling someone for a chat or, in extreme cases, getting out of bed. The reasoning behind it was that a small change in behaviour might elicit a process of positive change, and once they see the positive outcome of the changes, they would be more motivated to continue with it.

In positive psychology, only one wellbeing model includes a sense of accomplishment or, achievement, the PERMA model (Seligman, 2011). The explanation given for the inclusion of this component was associated with GRIT, which is the tendency to sustain long-term passion towards something and persevere through challenges (Duckworth et al., 2007) in other words, having a passion towards long-term goals (Von Culin et al., 2014). For example, children who have GRIT maintain their interest for a subject and continue working hard throughout the year, regardless of how many obstacles they come across. This is why GRIT mediated young people's deliberate practice at spelling bees (Duckworth et al., 2011) and predicted performance better than students' IQ (Duckworth, 2006).

Given that one of the components of GRIT is passion, it came to me as a surprise that there is no substantial research about the type of passion GRIT represents. The dualistic model of passion differentiates between obsessive passion and harmonious passion (Vallerand and Houlfort, 2003). Those who experience obsessive passion tend to down-regulate their positive emotions associated with winning, whereas harmoniously passionate people savour the moment (Schellenberg and Gaudreau, 2020). Obsessive passion prompts a lot of negative emotions, such as guilt about not training, when our passion is exercising, or shame if we don't do as well as we would like to. In contrast, harmonious passion is associated with positive emotions, as people who display it tend to control their urges towards the object they are passionate about and are well balanced in their approach to it. Not surprisingly, while both types of passion lead to accomplishments and achievements (Li, 2010), the obsessive passion reduces wellbeing, whereas the harmonious passion increases it (Vallerand et al., 2007). Given that GRIT is partially about passion, I couldn't understand why the dualistic model of passion is not explored in the GRIT literature.

Since there was no research about the obvious relationship between GRIT and passion, I asked some of my students to carry it out, as part of their Master's projects, which resulted in four separate studies that showed the same result: the passion that predicted GRIT was obsessive, meaning it is associated with negative experiences, not wellbeing. As it stands, I am not convinced that GRIT is a good representation of the component of accomplishment and would like to see more research carried out in this area.

Also, in a recent study with retiring high flyers, women who were in senior leadership positions and who were used to high levels of achievement and accomplishment at work, which was now missing from their retired lives, did not mention it as a direct source of their wellbeing (Kronsbein et al., n.d.). That said that accomplishment may have had an indirect effect on their wellbeing in that when we accomplish something we feel a sense of authentic pride. Let me explain this concept further.

There are two types of pride (Tracy and Robins, 2007). One is a hubristic pride, which refers to our global view of ourselves (e.g., I am a great person); and the second one, authentic pride, refers to our specific achievements (e.g., I am proud of my grade). Both types of pride are associated with different cognitive and affective processes associated with our attributions (Tracy and Robins, 2004). When we experience hubristic pride, we attribute our achievement to internal, stable and uncontrollable causes. What this means is that when we think "I am a great person," my *greatness* is associated with who I am, a mum, a dad, an employee, a student or our nationality. When someone criticise any aspect of my life, I am likely to take it personally.

On the other hand, when we experience authentic pride, we associate it with extrinsic, unstable and uncontrollable causes. For example, today I am proud of my grade, but tomorrow when my grade is lower, I do not change an opinion about myself. Because I associate my grade with hard work, rather than who I am, or I believe that if I work harder my grades will be better, meaning that I am in control of the factors that make me proud of myself. This way, pride makes me feel better more consistently. Hubristic pride often leads us astray and could potentially make us feel bad about ourselves. Authentic pride is the way to go.

When the two types of passion were measured across a lifespan (13–89 years old), hubristic pride systematically decreased from adolescence to midlife but then increased again into old age (Orth et al., 2010). However, authentic pride systematically increased across our lifespan and was also associated with an increase in education. This is why, it is possible that in the study with the retired high-flyers, an accomplishment may have been associated with them experiencing authentic pride, which in turn increased their wellbeing. This suggests that accomplishment may be indirectly associated with healthy pride.

Another important outcome of experiencing an accomplishment may be the feelings of higher self-esteem. Self-esteem in turn is associated with a variety of wellbeing factors, such as increased levels of positive affect, positive adjustment, better coping, resilience, or greater self-awareness (Carr, 2011). However, a study with children highlighted the danger of linking our accomplishments with our self-concept, given that some children conceptualised wellbeing through the lens of accomplishment, therefore, when they were not successful in their attempts, it was associated with symptoms of depression (Street et al., 2004). Therefore, accomplishment may have an indirect impact on a lot of processes that stimulate wellbeing, but care needs to be taken not to judge ourselves for our accomplishments, or lack thereof too much, and instead celebrate our incremental progress.

Interventions

Interventions for accomplishment may be as simple as setting up a goal and achieving it, which may give us a sense of accomplishment. However, in addition to this, we may also use savouring. *Savouring* is a process of appreciating what we have in our lives, which enhances our wellbeing (Bryant and Veroff, 2007). Savouring may happen across three time orientations, we can therefore reminisce about our past accomplishments, celebrate the present accomplishment or daydream about the future accomplishments. The authors identified ten strategies that help us savour. Firstly we can share our news with others, bringing us closer to people and creating a feeling of being supported by others. In a school community situation, this may be an announcement during a gathering, or on a website, or sharing the great things that have happened to us in the staff room. Secondly, it is about memory building, meaning that if something great happens, we try and remember this moment like a photograph, with all its glory. Comparing with someone who is worse off than us may improve our wellbeing. Comparing with someone who has accomplished more than us could reduce the feeling of wellness. Another strategy involves fully living through the moment, trying to intensify our emotions further. Absorption refers to recreating a state of flow, where we are fully engaged in the activity we savour. Tapping into our behavioural and physical expressions is yet another way to savour. In this case, we may dance, sing, laugh or jump up and down which will help us savour the moment kinaesthetically. Another technique involves acknowledging to oneself that time is short so we should live our lives to the full. This "carpe diem" thinking allows us to go wild into the savouring. The ninth strategy is by counting our blessings about the great fortune, our wonderful accomplishment. Finally, the tenth strategy is about what not to do, which is a kill-joy thinking encouraging ruminative thoughts. In addition to savouring, we may also help us feel more accomplished by setting up smart goals.

Autonomy and Control

I once heard someone describe teenagers as grown-ups with no control, because they are often asked to act as such, yet they are not permitted to drink, drive or have sex. I thought it was accurate, considering that adults tell them not only at what time to get up, but also when they are supposed to go to school, what they should wear, how they should behave in a classroom, when they can go to the toilet, eat, drink and when they are allowed to be merry. When young people listen to us and follow our lead, we are happy about this hassle-free relationship we have with them, and when they are children, we call them "good girl/boy." However, when they rebel against us, we get frustrated and desperately try to find another way to get them to do what we want them to do, even though deep in our hearts we know that rebelling is just their way of regaining a sense of control.

Regardless of our age, we need to feel in control (Cohen, 2012), which is why when a 5- year-old Bryan is taken to a nurse for a routine vaccination, he may scream and shout but sooner or later, the adults take control and make him have it. As soon as a he gets home and dries his tear-stained face, what does Bryan do? If he is like most kids, he probably takes one of his teddy bears and re-enacts the traumatic experience of being forced to accept a large needle piercing his leg. Yet, this time, it is Bryan who stabs the bear over and over again rationalising the pain he has felt. This is Bryan's way of regaining control.

Similar behaviours happen in a classroom. When Sam is berated by a teacher for not doing his homework, he acts out. It is his way of regaining control. When Jenny is forced to sit in the classroom for what seems like a lifetime, yearning to go home, she might be cranky on her way home drawing all her mother's attention, and finally controlling her life after a day of keeping quiet and not speaking up unless she is spoken to. Creating new avenues for control is just one thing we do in order to feel we are able to master our environment (Thompson and Wierson, 2000).

Another way in which we try to take control of our lives is by adjusting our goals. "I want to be a top readers in our class," "I want to get the top marks in maths," "I want to have plenty of friends in school." These are just some of the goals students may have when starting a new year. Yet, soon, if they are not performing as well as they want to, or if they are not achieving as much, they can either become disillusioned and helpless, leading them to feeling low or they might take the control back and reframe their goals. "What I really meant" they say "is that I want to be one of the top readers, get good marks in maths and have close friends, very good ones rather than plenty mediocre friends." When you hear children say that, you may think they are flaky, but what they have just done is regained a control over a situation which they found difficult to control.

The third way in which students take control of an uncontrollable situation is by accepting their circumstances. You may call it "giving up" but accepting circumstances is the difficult outcome of a long process of taking control. A student keeps trying to succeed in physics but is just not getting it. They get grinds, lower their expectations, act out and instead of thriving, they continue to barely reach the minimum requirement. What is their control-taking response to all this effort? "It's the most I can do in this subject. I'll never be really good at it, but it is ok, because I'm good at other stuff." Even though this attitude may seem like they are giving up, but they are actually taking control of their failures in order to feel like they are succeeding.

Why is taking control so important? Feeling in control is a significant part of wellbeing and a protective factor against developing helplessness (Seligman, 1975). Helplessness is feeling of inertia, passivity and surrendering to our circumstances. This means that an attempt to change is pointless; therefore, we get stuck in an unhappy place, from which we cannot see a way out. This is a state of acute lack of control, which becomes so debilitating that it may lead to depression.

The helplessness is not only depicted in our thoughts and feelings but also in our physical body. A chronic belief of being unable to control our environment is associated with increased reactivity to stress and lower immune functioning (Brosschot et al., 2006). This means that when experiencing a challenging situation, our stress levels grow to a point of destruction, whereas a person who feels in control is able to use stress to their advantage. Similarly, experiencing perpetually heightened levels of stress hinders our immune system to a degree where it does not protect us against illness to the same extent as before.

On the other hand, a feeling of control allows us to firstly determine what problems we are experiencing, and then engage our resources to solve them effectively (Ross and Mirowsky, 1989). Let me give you an example of how it worked in one of the schools I visited. Mark and Mary are math teachers in a large secondary school. Recently, the Department of Education brought in a policy, according to which the hours of teaching wellbeing needed to be increased. As a result, the school is in breach of the policy and the recent visit from the inspectorate saw a comment suggesting that 2 hours of math classes should be replaced with wellbeing classes in the next school year. Frustrated Mark felt out of control, so he found another avenue for taking control, which is venting in the staff room for the next few days and searching for job opportunities elsewhere. On the other hand, when Mary found out about the news, she sat down with Mark and brainstormed ideas on what alternatives they had. Together they came up with a list of suggestions which they brought to the attention of the principal. The principal took one of them on board, thus preventing the school from cutting the maths' hours in the forthcoming school year. Feeling in control is an important antecedent for identifying a problem and a subsequent solution.

In an educational context, feeling in control is associated with an increase in student achievement in schools (Collie et al., 2015). The more students feel in control of their studying, the better results they get. Psychologists call it an internal and external locus of control (Rotter, 1990). When students have an internal locus of control, they believe that they are able to control their environment. When they have predominantly an external locus of control, they believe that the environment controls them, and they don't have much say in it. This again can lead them to experiencing helplessness and disengagement.

Internal locus of control is also associated with positive emotions (Schrader and Nett, 2018). When young people engage in any activities that put them in the driving seat, be it a school activity or a pastime, such as playing computer games, their level of enjoyment increases and their level of frustration and anger decrease. On the other hand, when engaging in a similar activity that stripped them from control, their reactions are reversed.

A sense of control is one of the metacognitive skills that affects a lot of other things we do in life. When students learn how to regain control in a healthy and pro-social way by readjusting their goals, finding alternative avenues and accepting their circumstances, they use their skills to actively engage in enhancing their wellbeing. Having a perceived sense of control is such an important issue that schools may consider it for their wellbeing strategy.

Interventions

I recently taught a group of student-teachers aspiring to be leaders. They were experienced professionals used to having control in their lives, yet being students limited their control. In order to help them regain some of this control and feel better, I gave them an assignment with many choices, asked them to create study groups of their choice, requested they decide on a deadline and commit to it. I also gave them some additional topics for a lecture of their choice. The feedback I received from them was that it was the most enjoyable learning space they had experienced to date. By relinquishing some of my control, I have not only given them more control over their learning, but possibly higher levels of wellbeing. Schools may flip the power relations by introducing distributed leadership (Woods, 2016) used with teachers and students. Also, democratic leadership of the school and classroom is more likely to give students and teachers more autonomy over the decisions made in the school. This component of wellbeing is possibly one of the most powerful tools that schools have to boost their community's wellbeing and the great thing is that when it comes to control, letting go of small things matters.

Optimism

Whenever I ask teachers what optimism is, they usually tell me it's a wishful thinking. When I ask them how useful it is, they say it's not, as it lacks realism. When I probe further about the prevalence of optimism, they tell me that evolution theories taught them that human beings tend to be pessimistic, as it helps us survive danger, so pessimism, in most teachers' opinion, is more prevalent than optimism. When I tell them they are all incorrect in all their judgements, they usually laugh.

Optimism is not only useful, but necessary for survival (Seligman, 1990). It is about having an expectation that things will work out well for us in the future. When people do not have such an expectation, they tend to bury their head in the sand and avoid dealing with their issues, which is why pessimism is associated with denial, which leads to inertia (Carver et al., 2009). At the same time, optimists who are filled with an expectation that everything is going to work out well are more likely to take steps to influence their positive future. After all, there is nothing to fear if all is going to work out to their advantage anyway.

Some people claim that optimism is an unrealistic thinking. But so is pessimism, which claims that things will not work out well. Who are we to say that one way of thinking is more superior to another? Both are illusions, not realities. We all live in an illusion, regardless of whether we are pessimistic or optimistic thinkers. The question is whether our thinking is useful for us or not. Since optimism makes us more likely to survive and thrive, I tend to view it in the context of usefulness.

For many years, psychologists, such as Freud, Erikson, Maslow and Rogers, claimed that optimism was delusional (Peterson, 2000), which is why we did not study the merits of it until 1980s, when Shelley Taylor, a professor from Harvard University, turned our thinking on its head and showed us that positive expectancy is not only natural for us, but it is also necessary to help us cope with life adversities (Taylor, 1989). Taylor carried out research with groups of people who were terminally ill. When faced with potential death, most did not succumb to their illness, instead adapted a positive illusion and believed they would survive, despite the presence of disconfirming facts.

Two decades later, a neuroscientist revisited Taylor's research and found that indeed, most of us are optimistic, positively illusional and irrational in our view of the world (Sharot, 2011). However, the alternative is even more painful. Those who are not optimistically biased are at high risk of developing depression (Garrett and Sharot, 2017, Korn et al., 2014). Therefore, since optimism and pessimism are both illusions, it is a matter of choice as to which one serves us better.

There are currently two main theories of optimism: (1) Dispositional Optimism (Scheier and Carver, 1987) and (2) Explanatory Styles (Seligman, 1990). Dispositional optimism is further divided into trait and state optimism (Kluemper et al., 2009). However, since the explanatory style is a practical model that has already been applied robustly in education with promising results (Ma et al., 2020), I will explain this model in more detail and due to its complexity, I will try and simplify its terminology to make it more accessible.

An explanatory style refers to the way we explain our past positive and negative events in life. When experiencing adversity, such as failing a test, students who think optimistically tend to see this event as (1) temporary, believing that soon the bad times will finish and the good times will come back (pessimistic thinking: *Maths is too complicated, I'll never get it*; optimistic thinking: *I'm finding it difficult now, but if I study harder I will get better marks;* also, (2) they do not blame themselves solely for the adversity and consider external circumstances (pessimistic thinking: *it's all my fault, I'm useless*; optimistic thinking: *it's partially my fault, what influenced my test result was tiredness, as I studied all night. Next time, I need to get a better night sleep*) and (3) they are able to see the bad event in the context of their lives, which has both good and bad aspects to it (pessimistic thinking: *my life is ruined;* optimistic thinking: *I may have not done well in this test, but I did well in other subjects*). When explaining positive events, pessimistic and optimistic explanations are reversed.

Teaching children and adolescents optimism reduces their anxiety and depression for at least up 12 months (Brunwasser et al., 2009), and this is useful in overcoming adversity (Steinberg and Gano-Overway, 2003). In addition to protecting children, it also enhances their physical and mental health, and the effect on their wellbeing is long lasting (Wise and Rosqvist, 2006). Similar results apply to adults.

Interventions

One intervention, which is effective in turning around pessimistic thoughts, is the *ABCDE Disputation* (Seligman, 2002). A stands for an adverse event, meaning that we need to recall it along with the pessimistic thought we have experienced as a result of it (e.g., I will always be bullied). B stands for belief. At this stage, we need to write down our beliefs that are associated with the adverse event (e.g., I am no good, no wonder I am being bullied). C stands for consequences of our pessimistic thoughts (e.g., feeling suicidal). D stands for disputation (e.g., that's not fair, I don't deserve being bullied. I deserve being treated with dignity). E stands for energised, meaning that I'm energised and ready to change my thinking (e.g., I will speak to someone and the bullying will cease). This activity can be done on your own or in a group with children where they describe negative events that happened to them or a teacher works through a hypothetical situations and potential pessimistic thoughts associated with it. Also, teachers may try to *catch* students' pessimistic statements as they happen and ask them questions to challenge their pessimistic thinking. For younger children, activities that practice optimism include the match box from the *Bounce Back! Programme* (McGrath and Noble, 2017). Empty match boxes are stacked on top of each other. A teacher gently takes out one box from the stack, ensuring that the construction continues to stand strong, and says that this box represents a bad event in child's life, for example, a parent no longer living with them. Yet, even though the box is out, the scaffolding has remained strong because there are many great things going on in our lives that support us despite adversities.

Resilience

What is more detrimental to our health: daily hassles or traumatic events? The research shows that daily hassles may put more strain on our physical and mental health than some traumatic events (DeLongis et al., 1982). This may be due to the fact that they are relentless, often arrive unexpectedly, and we don't tend to give ourselves a break when experiencing daily hassles. On the other hand, traumatic events, such as bereavement, parental relationship dissolution or serious illness have a clear before and after the event boundaries. This helps us comprehend why we feel so bad, and often prompts us to take action to reduce the effect of trauma. More importantly, however, when experiencing traumatic events, we tend to receive more social support and are more likely to ask others for help, which is why dealing with daily hassles may put more strain on our health.

In a study with teachers, females scored higher on the number of daily hassles they experienced than their male colleagues (Vanitha and Husain, 2011). Their hassles included too much responsibility, travelling to and from work, not being able to say "No," not having enough time for their families and feeling like they are being taken for granted. Adolescents tend to react to daily hassles in a more pronounced way than younger children (Larson et al., 2002), even though their cognitive development and control tends to increase from childhood (Best and Miller, 2010). It may be due to the quantity of hassles they experience daily; getting up early in the morning, making sure that all their homework is done, going to classes, meeting with friends, potential conflicts and little dramas they may be experiencing in the midst of it all, which make daily hassles a nuisance.

The techniques we employ when managing both daily hassles and traumatic events depend on the level of resilience we have. There are over 100 definitions of resilience; however, broadly speaking, resilience includes an ability to manage our thoughts and emotions to an extent that we are not as affected by the event as much as someone who is less resilient (Davidson and Begley, 2012) and to bounce back or even grow after the event, thus enhancing their psychological wellbeing (Joseph and Hefferon, 2013).

According to a neuroscientist, our resilience is the ability of the prefrontal cortex (the area above our eye brows), which is responsible for executive thinking, to respond to a primal emotion created by the amygdala cells at the base of the brain (Davidson and Begley, 2012). More resilient people have developed well-travelled pathways between these parts of their brain, which allow this process to happen so rapidly that they may feel unaffected by adverse events. These well-developed pathways are outcomes of practice; therefore, resilience is something that we can all develop. Furthermore, research in schools suggests that developing resilience in children is effective and includes an amalgamation of many of the components discussed in this chapter, such as optimism, managing emotions or building supportive relationships (Ma et al., 2020).

Interventions

When we are effective in dealing with daily hassles, we employ a number of useful techniques. They include regulating our emotions, so that when we are anxious we are able to reframe it as excitement (Robertson, 2016) or engage in activities that turn our negative emotions into positive (Fredrickson, 2009). Alternatively, we may exercise our flexibility and adjust our goals to reduce self-directed negativity (Carver et al., 2014) or engage in self-regulatory behaviour, whereby we will manage our frustrations in an effective way (Stucke and Baumeister, 2006). All these techniques are helpful when coping with daily hassles.

In order to practice resilience, we can ask students to do the "*One door closes, another door opens*" activity, during which students are asked to recall situations when they lost something important to them, perhaps failed their test or were rejected by peers, and write or discuss how a door has opened shortly afterwards that allowed them to turn the negative event into positive (Rashid, 2008). Another intervention includes humour and is based on a *7 Humour Habits* Programme (Goldstein and Ruch, 2018), which endorses the following attitude and behaviour: (1) surround yourself with humour, (2) Cultivate a playful attitude, (3) Laugh more often and more heartily, (4) Create your own verbal humour, (5) Look for humour in everyday life, (6) Take yourself lightly: Laugh at yourself, (7) Find humour in the midst of stress.

Additional components

In this section, I will review some of the topics that may be included in a model of wellbeing specific to your school. They are not exhaustive, rather a few examples that I would consider when creating a wellbeing strategy for a school.

Physical health

Our mind is an integral part of our body. While it is important to keep our minds healthy, it is just as important to look after our body where our minds reside. If we don't eat well, for example, our glucose levels drop significantly, this will have a negative effect on our ability to manage our thoughts (Baumeister and Vohs, 2007), as we become more aggressive, less successful at difficult reasoning and thinking problems (Schmeichel et al., 2003). It also makes us selfish by putting our own needs first instead of considering the wellbeing of others (Balliet and Joireman, 2010). Reasoning and clear thinking are required if we want to be able to challenge negative thinking. This is just an example of why the physical aspect of wellbeing is often an added component to many of the wellbeing models in schools (Williams, 2011, Lai et al., 2018) and could perhaps become one of your components.

In 2010, 81% of adolescents worldwide failed to meet the World Health Organisation (WHO) recommendation of doing at least 60 min of moderate to vigorous physical activity (PA) daily (WHO, 2020). This is compared with adults of whom approximately a quarter reported being inactive in 2016. A longitudinal review of studies representing over 20,000 children aged 2–18 showed that over time, there is a decline in PA year-on-year from an early age (Abdulaziz et al., 2020). Therefore, we are growing a cohort of future inactive adults who may suffer the consequences of their sedentary lifestyles. PA is a wide-reaching term that describes any form of bodily movement (Caspersen et al., 1985). It includes exercise, which is a structured PA, walking to school, doing chores, walking the dog and many others, as long as they result in exerting energy.

There are many factors associated with young people's higher likelihood of engaging in PA. Contrary to the opinion that access to parks and playgrounds can facilitate children's engagement in PA, the results of several studies show inconsistency in this regard (Sterdt et al., 2014). However, the presence of transport infrastructure, such as an ability for young people to walk to school, rather than being dropped off, is associated with higher level of their PA (McMillan, 2005). Generally speaking, a shorter distance to school was associated with a tendency towards walking to school and higher level of PA (Cohen et al., 2006).

With regards to the school environment and a promotion of PA, creating a gym space for young people and exercise facilities made them more likely to engage in PA (Fein et al., 2004). It was true especially in schools where the equipment was available in the outdoor play area and adult supervision was supplemented with specific activity structures (Sallis et al., 2001). Another study found that painting the outdoor play areas with murals on the wall, snakes and ladders, basketball markings and similar was associated with higher numbers of students engaged in moderate and vigorous PA (Stratton and Mullan, 2005). At the same time, the weather and access to gym equipment at home had very little impact of young people's PA levels (Sterdt et al., 2014).

There are plenty of interventions that can be used to improve engagement with PA. *Dancing* is one of the most powerful interventions which boosts not only physical fitness and health but also psychological wellbeing (Connolly et al., 2011). Other interventions that may be organised in school are physical competitions, including 10,000 steps competitions for teams of teachers and parents outside of school. One of my colleagues, Dr Kate Hefferon, who specialises in the somatopsychic effect on wellbeing, introduced a stretch activity for all students, which they enjoyed so much that since then, every 20 min or so, I usually ask my students to stand up and stretch. After all, it is unnatural for us to stay in chairs motionless for too long. Also, setting up active homework during which students are asked to use PA and combine it with a development of their character strengths, is an effective intervention (Hefferon, 2013). For example, if the strength students want to develop is persistence, then their objective may be to set up a stretch-goal and persist through it. Alternatively, you may tweak this activity and ask the school community to practice one of the components of wellbeing during a PA. For instance, go for walks or runs together, if your wellbeing model includes positive relationships. Or find various ways to increase engagement when exercising, such as challenging yourself to allow you reach psychological flow. Other interventions may include the school's promotion of walking and cycling to school, for example, *Safe Routes to School* Programme (Boarnet et al., 2005) or using an m-health (mobile device) applications as they increase young people's awareness of the frequency of PA and help them incorporate PA in their daily routine more effectively (Carter et al., 2019). Finally, WHO has created some programmes that help students increase their PA and improve their eating habit levels. Whatever approach you select for your wellbeing strategy will be good as long as it gets young people and the rest of the school community moving and eating well.

Getting help

I spent a couple of years during my Ph.D. visiting secondary school students and helping them understand mood disorders, such as depression or anxiety. These sessions have lasted just over an hour and for many they were a starting point for realising they needed help. Increasing students' help-seeking behaviours in the event of a mental health issue is a very important first step towards making changes in their lives (Xu et al., 2018). After reviewing almost 100 studies that assessed the effectiveness of interventions for children as young as 2 years old, adolescents and adults , the researchers found that creating an awareness of the symptoms of pathologies, such as anxiety, depression, self-harm, substance abuse, and focussing on de-stigmatisation of the illness had a short-term effect on participants' willingness to seek help, meaning that perhaps it should be done on a more regular basis in school and a continuous part of the school strategy. When interventions that aimed to enhance participants' motivation to seek help were implemented, they were less effective short-term and more effective long-term, as people going through challenges needed the time to process what was happening to them. Also, approx. 70% of the interventions addressed parents, not children or adolescents, and there is a need to increase young people's knowledge of the symptoms and immobilise them to action, rather than depend on the adults to notice children's symptoms. This is particularly important given that many of us are so good at hiding our symptoms of mental distress.

In general, the wellbeing interventions presented in this book will be effective for preventing and coping with students' and teachers' anxiety (Brown et al., 2019), depression (Bolier et al., 2013) or eating disorders (Harrison et al., 2016). Some are also beneficial for alcohol-misusing adolescents (Akhtar and Boniwell, 2010) and groups with behavioural disorders (Ahmed and Boisvert, 2006). Therefore, if part of the wellbeing strategy in your school is to help people who experience mental health issues, apart from creating awareness by inviting specialists to discuss pathologies, your students with mental health issues may also participate in the activities you have designed for the healthy school community.

Stress Management

Over the years, the media have vilified stress. I remember going to training courses in the noughties and 2010s where the objective was to show us how bad stress is to us, because it raises our heart rate, increases the levels of cortisol and contributes to a lot of serious health problems. I remember that at the time, it didn't really make sense to me, because I have experienced that raised heart rate every day at work and not only did I not consider it stressful, but I kind of enjoyed it. My colleagues used to tell me that I was an adrenaline junkie, but this couldn't be further from the truth. This is why, years later I welcomed the studies that came from Prof. Ian Robertson (Robertson, 2016), a neuropsychologist who found that what we consider stress and excitement look the same on brain scans.

When we are stressed we experience a chemical cocktail of endorphins, adrenaline, testosterone and dopamine which give us more motivation, a feeling of rush, sense of confidence and the feeling similar to that observed in people who are in love or skydivers falling out of plane (Allison et al., 2012). When we are excited or stressed, we experience a similar reaction from the physiological perspective, the only difference is our interpretation of it (Robertson, 2016). When we think we are getting thrilling excitement, we are even more motivated by these feelings, when we think it's debilitating stress, we become tired, perhaps more negative and aim to withdraw from the situation.

Yet, if only we saw all these physiological reactions as helpful, instead of harmful, our attitude towards them would be more welcoming. After all, when we are facing a challenging situation, the liver drops fat and sugar into our bloodstream to provide our bodies with more fuel; breathing deepens so that more oxygen is delivered to our heart and our heart rate speeds up to deliver that oxygen as quickly as possible to our brain and muscles (McGonigal, 2016). The purpose of all this is to help us gain energy and think more clearly, so that we can cope with this challenge more effectively. This is important: our bodies under physiological stress help us, not hinder us, to tackle a challenge.

Unfortunately, over the years, we have learnt that these physiological reactions that are associated with stress are bad for us; therefore, our attitude towards stress has become negative. When we search "stress" online, images of the negative effect of distress pop up, instead of positive images of how helpful stress can be to us. These consequences of distress paint an incorrect picture of the situation. When we experience stress for a long time or cope with it through denial, it is indeed detrimental to our health; however, the stressful physiological reaction to a challenge is just a sign for us to engage in a coping behaviour, and an immobilisation for our body to tackle the situation. This is nothing to be afraid of.

The study that profoundly changed the way we view stress is one that researched almost 30,000 people in the USA (Keller et al., 2012). They asked people about their attitude towards stress, as well as the amount of stress they experienced. Then, 8 years later, the researchers went through the mortality data to find out who from the group had died and came up with some striking findings. Of those who had experienced a lot of stress and believed that stress was harmful to them, their risk of dying increased by 43%; for those who experienced a little stress but still believed it to be harmful to them, their risk of dying increased by 10%; however, surprisingly, those who experienced a lot of stress, like the first group, but did not believe it to be harmful to them, increased their risk of dying by just 8.3%.

This study showed us that it is not only the amount of stress we experience that matters but also the attitude we have towards it. That attitude changes our behaviour, alters the way in which we cope with stress, which is why the results of this study showed a stark difference between these groups. When we consider stress as harmful, we are more likely to bury our heads in the sand, go into denial about it and deal with the symptoms of stress rather than identify the source of it and fix it (McGonigal, 2016). On the other hand, when we are open towards stress and see it as helpful at times, we are more likely to face the challenge head-on and become more proactive about resolving it, fixing the problem and asking others for help. All these behaviours make a significant difference to our outcomes.

The good news is that in the same way that we have learnt to fear stress, we can unlearn this attitude and subsequent behaviour. I carried out an experiment with a group of 849 adults (Burke, 2018). They were invited to attend a 3-hour training session, during which I introduced them to both the negative and positive effects of stress, some negative thoughts that are not useful in a stressful situation and positive thoughts we could replace them with. We then discussed some practical ways that we can cope with stress more effectively. I asked the group to complete a stress-mindset questionnaire before the session and immediately after. What I found was that prior to the session, 23.6% of participants believed that stress is harmful to them, after the session, only 3.1% of them believed the same, meaning that 96.9% of participants did not see stress as being harmful anymore. This change in attitude hallmarks behavioural changes (McGonigal, 2016). When I followed up with the group a year later, some claimed that the session was life-changing for them and changed their attitude and behaviour to such an extent that people around have commented on their transformation.

Stress mindset has been measured in adolescents at the beginning and end of the school year (Park et al., 2018). An increase of adverse situations during the school year was usually associated with increases in students' perceived stress and decreases in their level of self-control. However, when adolescents believed that stress is helpful to them, not harmful, they were less likely to perceive stress after experiencing adverse situations. We need more research into the effect of stress mindset on young people in the face of school-related challenges. But these preliminary findings show that teaching young people this positive attitude towards stress is possibly one of the most promising interventions we can use to help them cope with stressful events, such as class tests or school exams.

In order for schools to teach this new attitude, it is important that teachers take it on board too. To date, there is only a handful of research papers relating to stress mindset in schools. One study, found that stress mindset predicted both teachers' stress levels and their job turnover (Kim et al., 2020). This is confirmed in non-teacher-related research showing that stress as an enhancing mindset led to experiencing less distress, depression, anxiety and improved levels of energy (Crum et al., 2013). This also led to more adaptive behaviours, such as putting more effort into planning and scheduling and when individuals experience heavy workload and trying to see this as a learning-opportunity (Casper et al., 2017). Given that according to the Gallup organisation, 46% of teachers in K-12 settings report high levels of daily stress during the school year (Gallup, 2014), teaching teachers the stress-is-enhancing mindset can help them cope with work-related stress more effectively.

School community

Despite most of the components discussed in this chapter relating to individuals, it is important to remember that when implemented as a school community's intervention they will make a bigger impact on students, teachers and parents. Also, they need to be age-appropriate; therefore, while I have mentioned a few interventions for younger children, they would need to be tweaked by the committee to apply in primary schools. What is important is that the foundations of the components will remain, while the only change we will see is how they are introduced to young people.

Take-aways for the school's wellbeing strategy

- There are many wellbeing components you can include in your wellbeing strategy.
- Consider which ones can add the biggest value to your school community.
- Use the components to design your school's wellbeing framework.

References

Abdulaziz, F., Martin, A., Janssen, X., Wilson, M.G., Gibson, A., Hughes, A. & Reilly, J.J. 2020. "Longitudinal Changes in Moderate-to-vigorous-intensity Physical Activity in Children and Adolescents: A Systematic Review and Meta-analysis." *Obesity Reviews* 21 (1).

Ahmed, E. & Braithwaite, V. 2006. Forgiveness, reconciliation, and shame: Three key variables in reducing school bullying. *Journal of Social Issues*, 62, 347–370.

Ahmed, M. & Boisvert, C. M. 2006. Using positive psychology with special mental health populations. *American Psychologist*, 61, 333–335.

Akhtar, M. & Boniwell, I. 2010. Applying positive psychology to alcohol-misusing adolescents: A group intervention. *Groupwork: An Interdisciplinary Journal for Working with Groups*, 20, 6–31.

Akhtar, S. & Barlow, J. 2018. Forgiveness therapy for the promotion of mental well-being: A systematic review and meta-analysis. *Trauma, Violence, & Abuse*, 19, 107–122.

Akos, P. & Kurz, M. S. 2016. Applying hope theory to support middle school transitions. *Middle School Journal*, 47, 13–18.

Akpan, P. L. & Saunders, P. J. 2017. From shame to mindfulness and self-compassion: A teacher's journey to greater self-efficacy. *Journal of the International Society for Teacher Education*, 21, 41–49.

Algoe, S. B., Haidt, J. & Gable, S. L. 2008. Beyond reciprocity: Gratitude and relationships in everyday life. *Emotion*, 8, 425–429.

Allen, K., Kern, M. L., Vella-Brodrick, D., Hattie, J. & Waters, L. 2018. What schools need to know about fostering school belonging: A meta-analysis. *Educational Psychology Review*, 30, 1–34.

Allen, K.-A., Kern, M. L., Vella-Brodrick, D. & Waters, L. 2017. School values: A comparison of academic motivation, mental health promotion, and school belonging with student achievement. *Educational and Developmental Psychologist*, 34, 31–47.

Allison, A. L., Peres, J. C., Boettger, C., Leonbacher, U., Hastings, P. D. & Shirtcliff, E. A. 2012. Fight, flight, or fall: Autonomic nervous system reactivity during skydiving. *Personality and Individual Differences*, 53, 218–223.

Ascioglu Onal, A. & Yalcin, I. 2017. Forgiveness of others and self-forgiveness: The predictive role of cognitive distortions, empathy, and rumination. *Eurasian Journal of Educational Research*, 97–120.

Askell-Williams, H. 2016. Parents' perspectives of school mental health promotion initiatives are related to parents' self-assessed parenting capabilities. *Journal of Psychologists and Counsellors in Schools*, 26, 16–34.

Austin, D. B. 2005. *The effects of a strengths development intervention program upon the self-perceptions of students' academic abilities.* 66, ProQuest Information & Learning.

Averill, J. R., Catlin, G. & Chon, K. K. 1990. *Rules of hope.* New York, NY: Springer-Verlag Publshing.

Balliet, D. & Joireman, J. 2010. Ego depletion reduces proselfs' concern with the well-being of others. *Group Processes & Intergroup Relations*, 13, 227–239.

Barbuto, J. E., Jr. & Bugenhagen, M. J. 2009. The emotional intelligence of leaders as antecedent to leader-member exchanges: A field study. *Journal of Leadership Education*, 8, 135–146.

Baumeister, R. F. & Vohs, K. D. 2007. Self-regulation, ego depletion, and motivation. *Social and Personality Psychology Compass*, 1, 115–128.

Beck, J. S. 2011. *Cognitive behavior therapy: Basics and beyond.* New York: The Guilford Press.

Benarous, X. & Munch, G. 2016. Inside children's emotions: Thoughts on Pixar's Inside Out. *Journal of Developmental and Behavioral Pediatrics*, 37, 522–522.

Best, J. R. & Miller, P. H. 2010. A developmental perspective on executive function. *Child Development*, 81, 1641–1660.

Bharara, G. 2019. Factors facilitating a positive transition to secondary school: A systematic literature review. *International Journal of School & Educational Psychology*.

Boarnet, M. G., Day, K. & Anderson, C. 2005. California's safe routes to school program. *Journal of the American Planning Association*, 71, 301–317.

Bolier, L., Haverman, M., Westerhof, G. J., Riper, H., Smit, F. & Bohlmeijer, E. 2013. Positive psychology interventions: A meta-analysis of randomized controlled studies. *BMC Public Health*, 13, 1–20.

Boniwell, I. & Tunariu, A. D. 2019. *Positive psychology theory, research and applications.* London: Open University Press.

Bono, G., Mccullough, M. E. & Root, L. M. 2008. Forgiveness, feeling connected to others, and well-being: Two longitudinal studies. *Personality and Social Psychology Bulletin*, 34, 182–195.

Brewin, C. R. & Lennard, H. 1999. Effects of mode of writing on emotional narratives. *Journal of Traumatic Stress*, 12, 355.

Brosschot, J. F., Gerin, W. & Thayer, J. F. 2006. The perseverative cognition hypothesis: A review of worry, prolonged stress-related physiological activation, and health. *Journal of Psychosomatic Research*, 60, 113–124.

Brown, L., Ospina, J. P., Celano, C. M. & Huffman, J. C. 2019. The effects of positive psychological interventions on medical patients' anxiety: A meta-analysis. *Psychosomatic Medicine*, 81, 595–602.

Brunwasser, S. M., Giliham, J. E. & Kim, E. S. 2009. A meta-analytic review of the Penn resiliency program's effect on depressive symptoms. *Journal of Consulting & Clinical Psychology*, 77, 1042–1054.

Brunzell, T., Stokes, H. & Waters, L. 2018. Why do you work with struggling students? Teacher perceptions of meaningful work in trauma-impacted classrooms. *Australian Journal of Teacher Education*, 43, 116–142.

Bryant, F. B. & Veroff, J. 2007. *Savoring: A new model of positive experience.* Mahwah, NJ: Lawrence Erlbaum Associates Publishers.

Burke, J. 2017. *Happiness after 30: The paradox of aging.*, Dublin, Jumpp Publishing.

Burke, J. 2018. Turning stress into positive energy: An evaluation of a workplace intervention. *Positive Work and Organizations: Research and Practice*.

Burke, J. & McGuckin, C. in press. Bullying and character development: An examination of character strengths associated with bullying and cyberbullying in post-primary schools in Ireland. *Journal of Character Education*.

Burton, C. M. & King, L. A. 2004. The health benefits of writing about intensely positive experiences. *Journal of Research in Personality*, 38, 150–163.

Carr, A. 2011. *Positive psychology: The science of happiness and human strengths*, 2nd ed. New York, NY: Routledge/Taylor & Francis Group.

Carter, D., Robinson, K., Forbes, J. & Hayes, S. 2019. 79 physical activity promotion using mhealth: A systematic review and meta-synthesis of adults' experiences. *Age & Ageing*, 48, iii1–iii16.

Carver, C. S., Scheier, M. F., Miller, C. J. & Fulford, D. 2009. Optimism. In: Lopez, S. J. & Snyder, C. R. (eds.), *Oxford handbook of positive psychology*, 2nd ed. New York, NY: Oxford University Press.

Carver, C. S., Scheier, M. F. & Johnson, S. L. 2014. Origins and functions of positive affect: A goal regulation perspective. In: Gruber, J. & Moskowitz, J. T. (eds.), *Positive emotion: Integrating the light sides and dark sides*. New York, NY: Oxford University Press.

Casper, A., Sonnentag, S. & Tremmel, S. 2017. Mindset matters: The role of employees' stress mindset for day-specific reactions to workload anticipation. *European Journal of Work & Organizational Psychology*, 26, 798–810.

Caspersen, C. J., Powell, K. E. & Christenson, G. M. 1985. Physical activity, exercise, and physical fitness: Definitions and distinctions for health-related research. *Public Health Reports*, 100, 126–131.

Cejudo, J., López-Delgado, M. L. & Losada, L. 2019. Effectiveness of the videogame "Spock" for the improvement of the emotional intelligence on psychosocial adjustment in adolescents. *Computers in Human Behavior*, 101, 380–386.

Chaplin, T. M. & Aldao, A. 2013. Gender differences in emotion expression in children: A meta-analytic review. *Psychological Bulletin*, 139, 735–765.

Cheung, C. S. 2019. Parents' involvement and adolescents' school adjustment: Teacher–student relationships as a mechanism of change. *School Psychology*, 34, 350–362.

Chu, S. T.-W. & Mak, W. W. S. 2019. How mindfulness enhances meaning in life: A meta-analysis of correlational studies and randomized controlled trials. *Mindfulness*, 11, 177–193.

Cohen, D. A., Ashwood, S., Scott, M., Overton, A., Evenson, K. R., Voorhees, C. C., Bedimo-Rung, A. & Mckenzie, T. L. 2006. Proximity to school and physical activity among middle school girls: The trial of activity for adolescent girls study. *Journal of Physical Activity & Health*, 3, S129–S138.

Cohen, L. J. 2012. *Playful parenting*. USA: Ballantine Books.

Collie, R. J., Martin, A. J., Malmberg, L. E., Hall, J. & Ginns, P. 2015. Academic buoyancy, student's achievement, and the linking role of control: A cross-lagged analysis of high school students. *British Journal of Educational Psychology*, 85, 113–130.

Compas, B. E., Jaser, S. S., Bettis, A. H., Watson, K. H., Gruhn, M. A., Dunbar, J. P., Williams, E. & Thigpen, J. C. 2017. Coping, emotion regulation, and psychopathology in childhood and adolescence: A meta-analysis and narrative review. *Psychological Bulletin*, 143, 939–991.

Connolly, M. K., Quin, E. & Redding, E. 2011. Dance 4 your life: Exploring the health and well-being implications of a contemporary dance intervention for female adolescents. *Research in Dance Education*, 12, 53–66.

Crum, A. J., Salovey, P. & Achor, S. 2013. Rethinking stress: The role of mindsets in determining the stress response. *Journal of Personality and Social Psychology*, 104, 716–733.

Csikszentmihalyi, M. 1997. *Creativity: Flow and the psychology of discovery and invention*. New York, NY: HarperCollins Publishers.

Csikszentmihalyi, M. 2009. Flow. In: Lopez, S. (ed.), *The encyclopedia of positive psychology*. Chichester: Blackwell Publishing Ltd.

Curry, O. S., Rowland, L. A., Van Lissa, C. J., Zlotowitz, S., Mcalaney, J. & Whitehouse, H. 2018. Happy to help? A systematic review and meta-analysis of the effects of performing acts of kindness on the well-being of the actor. *Journal of Experimental Social Psychology*, 76, 320–329.

Davidson, R. J. & Begley, S. 2012. *The emotional life of your brain.*, London, Hodder & Stoughton.

Delongis, A., Coyne, J. C., Dakof, G., Folkman, S. & Lazarus, R. S. 1982. Relationship of daily hassles, uplifts, and major life events to health status. *Health Psychology*, 1, 119–136.

Demanet, J. & Van Houtte, M. 2012. School belonging and school misconduct: The differing role of teacher and peer attachment. *Journal of Youth & Adolescence*, 41, 499–514.

Diebel, T., Woodcock, C., Cooper, C. & Brignell, C. 2016. Establishing the effectiveness of a gratitude diary intervention on children's sense of school belonging. *Educational & Child Psychology*, 33, 117–129.

Digdon, N. & Koble, A. 2011. Effects of constructive worry, imagery distraction, and gratitude interventions on sleep quality: A pilot trial. *Applied Psychology: Health & Well-Being*, 3, 193–206.

Dorroh, J. 1993. Reflections on expressive writing in the science class. *Quarterly of the National Writing Project and the Center for the Study of Writing and Literacy.*

Duckworth, A. L. 2006. *Intelligence is not enough: Non-IQ predictors of achievement.* 67, ProQuest Information & Learning, University of Pennsylvania, Ph.d dissertation.

Duckworth, A. L., Peterson, C., Matthews, M. D. & Kelly, D. R. 2007. Grit: Perseverance and passion for long-term goals. *Journal of Personality and Social Psychology*, 92, 1087–1101.

Duckworth, A. L., Kirby, T. A., Tsukayama, E., Berstein, H. & Ericsson, K. A. 2011. Deliberate practice spells success: Why grittier competitors triumph at the National Spelling Bee. *Social Psychological and Personality Science*, 2, 174–181.

Dunleavy, G. & Burke, J. 2019. Fostering a sense of belonging at an international school in France: An experimental study. *Educational & Child Psychology*, 36, 34–45.

Edgar-Smith, S. & Palmer, R. B. 2017. Alternative school student perceptions about forgiveness. *Preventing School Failure*, 61, 259–267.

Ekman, P. 2004. *Emotions revealed: Understanding faces and feelings.* London: Phoenix.

Emmons, R. A. & Mccullough, M. E. 2003. Counting blessings versus burdens: An experimental investigation of gratitude and subjective well-being in daily life. *Journal of Personality and Social Psychology*, 84, 377–389.

B A Esterling, L L'Abate, E J Murray, J W Pennebaker 2001. Empirical foundations for writing in prevention and psychotherapy: Mental and physical health. *Advances in Mind-Body Medicine*, 17, 60.

Fahlman, S. A., Mercer-Lynn, K. B., Flora, D. B. & Eastwood, J. D. 2013. Development and validation of the multidimensional state boredom scale. *Assessment*, 20, 68–85.

Fehr, R. & Gelfand, M. J. 2012. The forgiving organization: A multilevel model of forgiveness at work. *Academy of Management Review*, 37, 664–688.

Fein, A. J., Plotnikoff, R. C., Wild, T. C. & Spence, J. C. 2004. Perceived environment and physical activity in youth. *International Journal of Behavioral Medicine*, 11, 135–142.

Finlay-Jones, A. L. 2017. The relevance of self-compassion as an intervention target in mood and anxiety disorders: A narrative review based on an emotion regulation framework. *Clinical Psychologist*, 21, 90–103.

Fredrickson, B. L. 2001. The role of positive emotions in positive psychology: The broaden-and-build theory of positive emotions. *American Psychologist*, 56, 218–226.

Fredrickson, B. L. 2009. *Positivity: Top-notch research reveals the 3-to-1 ratio that will change your life.*, New York, Mfj Books.

Fredrickson, B. L. 2013. *Love 2.0: Finding Happiness and Health in Moments of Connection*, London, UK, Penguin Group.

Fredrickson, B. L. & Joiner, T. 2002. Positive emotions trigger upward spirals toward emotional well-being. *Psychological Science* 13: 172 (0956–7976).

Fredrickson, B. L. & Joiner, T. 2018. Reflections on positive emotions and upward spirals. *Perspectives on Psychological Science*, 13, 194–199.

Fredrickson, B. L., Tugade, M. M. & Waugh, C. E. 2003. What good are positive emotions in crises? A prospective study of resilience and emotions following the terrorist attacks on the united states on september 11th, 2001. *Journal of Personality & Social Psychology*, 84, 365–376.

Fredrickson, B. L., Cohn, M. A., Coffey, K. A., Pek, J. & Finkel, S. M. 2008. Open hearts build lives: Positive emotions, induced through loving-kindness meditation, build consequential personal resources. *Journal of Personality and Social Psychology*, 95, 1045–1062.

Freeman, T. M., Anderman, L. H. & Jensen, J. M. 2007. Sense of belonging in college freshmen at the classroom and campus levels. *Journal of Experimental Education*, 75, 203–220.

Freire, T. *Optimal experience in Portugense adolescents: the role of the school context*. European Conference on Positive Psychology, 2004 Verbania, Italy.

Freire, T., Lima, I., Teixeira, A., Araújo, M. R. & Machado, A. 2018. Challenge: To be+ A group intervention program to promote the positive development of adolescents. *Children and Youth Services Review*, 87, 173–185.

Frisch, M. B. 2006. *Quality of Life Therapy: Applying a life satisfaction approach to positive psychology and cognitive therapy*, New York, NY, John Wiley & Sons Ltd.

Froh, J. J., Kashdan, T. B., Ozimkowski, K. M. & Miller, N. 2009. Who benefits the most from a gratitude intervention in children and adolescents? Examining positive affect as a moderator. *The Journal of Positive Psychology*, 4, 408–422.

Gable, S. L., Reis, H. T., Impett, E. A. & Asher, E. R. 2004. What do you do when things go right? The intrapersonal and interpersonal benefits of sharing positive events. *Journal of Personality and Social Psychology*, 87, 228–245.

Gallup 2014. *State of America's schools: The path to winning again in education* [Online]. Available: https://www.gallup.com/education/269648/state-america-schools-report.aspx. [Accessed: 23rd Sep 2020].

García-Alandete, J., Rosa Martínez, E., Sellés Nohales, P. & Soucase Lozano, B. 2018. Meaning in life and psychological well-being in Spanish emerging adults. *Acta Colombiana de Psicología*, 21, 196–205.

Garland, E. L., Fredrickson, B., Kring, A. M., Johnson, D. P., Meyer, P. S. & Penn, D. L. 2010. Upward spirals of positive emotions counter downward spirals of negativity: Insights from the broaden-and-build theory and affective neuroscience on the treatment of emotion dysfunctions and deficits in psychopathology. *Clinical Psychology Review*, 30, 849–864.

Garrett, N. & Sharot, T. 2017. Optimistic update bias holds firm: Three tests of robustness following Shah et al. *Consciousness and Cognition: An International Journal*, 50, 12–22.

Geraghty, A. W. A., Wood, A. M. & Hyland, M. E. 2010. Attrition from self-directed interventions: Investigating the relationship between psychological predictors, intervention content and dropout from a body dissatisfaction intervention. *Social Science & Medicine*, 71, 30–37.

Gersten, R. & Baker, S. 2001. Teaching expressive writing to students with learning disabilities: A meta-analysis. *Elementary School Journal*, 101, 551–572.

Glasser, W. 1999. *Choice theory: A new psychology of personal freedom*, New York, NY, HarperPerennial.

Goldstein, J. & Ruch, W. 2018. Paul McGhee and humor research. *Humor: International Journal of Humor Research*, 31, 169–181.

Goodenow, C. 1993. Classroom belonging among early adolescent students: Relationships to motivation and achievement. *The Journal of Early Adolescence*, 13, 21–43.

Govindji, R. & Linley, P. 2008. An evaluation of celebrating strengths. *Prepared for North Lincolnshire Local Education Authority*. Coventry: CAPP, Warwick University.

Greenberg, M. A. 2008. Emotional storytelling after stressful experiences. In: Lopez, S. J. (ed.), *Positive psychology: Exploring the best in people, Vol. 3: Growing in the face of adversity*. Westport, CT: Praeger Publishers/Greenwood Publishing Group.

Greif, E. B. & Gleason, J. B. 1980. Hi, Thanks, and Goodbye: More Routine Information. *Language in Society*, 9, 159–166.

Harrison, A., AL-Khairulla, H. & Kikoler, M. 2016. The feasibility, acceptability and possible benefit of a positive psychology intervention group in an adolescent inpatient eating disorder service. *The Journal of Positive Psychology*, 11, 449–459.

Harzer, C. & Ruch, W. 2012. When the job is a calling: The role of applying one's signature strengths at work. *Journal of Positive Psychology*, 7, 362–371.

Harzer, C. & Ruch, W. 2016. Your strengths are calling: Preliminary results of a web-based strengths intervention to increase callin. *Journal of Happiness Studies*, 17, 2237–2256.

Haslip, M. J., Allen-Handy, A. & Donaldson, L. 2019. How do children and teachers demonstrate love, kindness and forgiveness? Findings from an early childhood strength-spotting intervention. *Early Childhood Education Journal*, 47, 531–547.

Hauser, M. D. 2018. The mind of a goal achiever: Using mental contrasting and implementation intentions to achieve better outcomes in general and special education. *Mind, Brain, and Education*, 12, 102–109.

Hefferon, K. 2013. *Positive psychology and the body: The somatopsychic side to flourishing*, Maindenhead, UK, Open University Press.

Hefferon, K. & Boniwell, I. 2011. *Positive psychology theory research and applications*, Berkshire, UK, Open University Press.

Heintzelman, S. & King, L. A. 2014. Life is pretty meaningful. *American Psychologist*, 69, 561–574.

Hektner, J. M. & Csikszentmihalyi, M. 1996. *A Longitudinal Exploration of Flow and Intrinsic Motivation in Adolescents. Paper presented at the Annual Meeting of the American Educational Research Association*, New York.

Hemmings, B., Kay, R. & Sharp, J. G. 2019. The relationship between academic trait boredom, learning approach and university achievement. *Educational and Developmental Psychologist*, 36, 41–50.

Hershfield, H. E., Scheibe, S., Sims, T. L., & Carstensen, L. L. (2013). When feeling bad can be good: Mixed emotions benefit physical health across adulthood. *Social Psychological and Personality Science*, 4(1), 54–61.

Hicks, J. A. & King, L. A. 2009. Positive mood and social relatedness as information about meaning in life. *Journal of Positive Psychology*, 4, 471–482.

Hill, J. *How well do we know our strengths? British Psychological Society Centenary Conference*, 2001 Glasgow, Scotland.

Hoggard, L. 2005. *How to be happy*, London, BBC Books.

Hone, L. C., Jarden, A., Duncan, S. & Schofield, G. M. 2015. Flourishing in New Zealand workers. *Journal of Occupational & Environmental Medicine*, 57, 973–983.

Houri, A. K., Thayer, A. J. & Cook, C. R. 2019. Targeting parent trust to enhance engagement in a school–home communication system: A double-blind experiment of a parental wise feedback intervention. *School Psychology*, 34, 421–432.

Howells, K. 2014. An exploration of the role of gratitude in enhancing teacher–student relationships. *Teaching and Teacher Education*, 42, 58–67.

Huffman, J. C., Dubois, C. M., Healy, B. C., Boehm, J. K., Kashdan, T. B., Celano, C. M., Denninger, J. W. & Lyubomirsky, S. 2014. Feasibility and utility of positive psychology exercises for suicidal inpatients. *General Hospital Psychiatry*, 36, 88–94.

Isham, A., Gatersleben, B. & Jackson, T. 2019. Flow activities as a route to living well with less. *Environment and Behavior*, 51, 431–461.

Joiner, T. 2005. *Why people die by suicide*, Cambridge, MA, Harvard University Press.

Joseph, S. & Hefferon, K. 2013. Post-traumatic growth: Eudaimonic happiness in the aftermath of adversity. In: David, S. A., Boniwell, I. & Conley Ayers, A. (eds.), *The Oxford handbook of happiness*. New York, NY: Oxford University Press.

Kahneman, D., Krueger, A. B., Schkade, D. A., Schwarz, N. & Stone, A. A. 2004. A survey method for characterizing daily life experience: The day reconstruction method. *Science*, 306, 1776–1780.

Keller, A., Litzelman, K., Wisk, L. E., Maddox, T., Cheng, E. R., Creswell, P. D. & Witt, W. P. W. W. E. 2012. Does the perception that stress affects health matter? The association with health and mortality. *Health Psychology*, 31, 677–684.

Keyes, C. L. M. 2002. The exchange of emotional support with age and its relationship with emotional well-being by age. *The Journals of Gerontology: Series B: Psychological Sciences and Social Sciences*, 57, P518–P525.

Kim, H. & Niederdeppe, J. 2013. The role of emotional response during an H1N1 influenza pandemic on a college campus. *Journal of Public Relations Research*, 25, 30–50.

Kim, J., Shin, Y., Tsukayama, E. & Park, D. 2020. Stress mindset predicts job turnover among preschool teachers. *Journal of School Psychology*, 78, 13–22.

Kim, Y. 2008. Effects of expressive writing among bilinguals: Exploring psychological well-being and social behaviour. *British Journal of Health Psychology*, 13, 43–47.

King, L. A. 2001. The health benefits of writing about life goals. *Personality and Social Psychology Bulletin*, 27, 798–807.

King, L. A. & Miner, K. N. 2000. Writing about the perceived benefits of traumatic events: Implications for physical health. *Personality and Social Psychology Bulletin*, 26, 220–230.

Kluemper, D. H., Little, L. M. & Degroot, T. 2009. State or trait: effects of state optimism on job-related outcomes. *Journal of Organizational Behavior*, 30, 209–231.

Kok, B. E., Coffey, K. A., Cohn, M. A., Catalino, L. I., Vacharkulksemsuk, T., Algoe, S. B., Brantley, M. & Fredrickson, B. L. 2013. How positive emotions build physical health: Perceived positive social connections account for the upward spiral between positive emotions and vagal tone. *Psychological Science*, 24, 1123–1132.

Korn, C. W., Sharot, T., Walter, H., Heekeren, H. R. & Dolan, R. J. 2014. Depression is related to an absence of optimistically biased belief updating about future life events. *Psychological Medicine*, 44, 579–592.

Kronsbein, K., Belovsky, M. & Burke, J. n.d. forthcoming. Retired high-flyers: Exploring the impact of accomplishment on wellbeing in retired female Ceos.

Lai, M. K., Leung, C., Kwok, S. Y. C., Hui, A. N. N., Lo, H. H. M., Leung, J. T. Y. & Tam, C. H. L. 2018. A multidimensional Perma-H positive education model, general satisfaction of school life, and character strengths use in Hong Kong senior primary school students: Confirmatory factor analysis and path analysis using the Apaso-II. *Frontiers in Psychology*, 9: 1099.

Lambert, N. M., Stillman, T. F., Hicks, J. A., Kamble, S., Baumeister, R. F. & Fincham, F. D. 2013. To belong is to matter: Sense of belonging enhances meaning in life. *Personality and Social Psychology Bulletin*, 39, 1418–1427.

Larsen J.T., Hemenover S.H., Norris C.J., Cacioppo J.T. 2003. Turning adversity to advantage: On the virtues of the coactivation of positive and negative emotions. In: Aspinwall LG, Staudinger UM, editors. *A psychology of human strengths: Perspectives on an emerging field*. 211-226 Washington, DC: American Psychological Association.

Larson, R. W., Moneta, G., Richards, M. H. & Wilson, S. 2002. Continuity, stability, and change in daily emotional experience across adolescence. *Child Development*, 73, 1151–1165.

Layous, K., Chancellor, J. & Lyubomirsky, S. 2014. Positive activities as protective factors against mental health conditions. *Journal of Abnormal Psychology*, 123, 3–12.

Lazarus, R. S. 1999. Hope: An Emotion and a Vital Coping Resource Against Despair. *Social Research*, 66, 653–678.

Leary, M. R., Tate, E. B., Adams, C. E., Batts Allen, A. & Hancock, J. 2007. Self-compassion and reactions to unpleasant self-relevant events: The implications of treating oneself kindly. *Journal of Personality and Social Psychology*, 92, 887–904.

Li, C.-H. 2010. Predicting subjective vitality and performance in sports: The role of passion and achievement goals. *Perceptual and Motor Skills*, 110, 1029–1047.

Li, J.-B., Dou, K. & Liang, Y. 2020. The relationship between presence of meaning, search for meaning, and subjective well-being: A three-level meta-analysis based on the meaning in life questionnaire. *Journal of Happiness Studies: An Interdisciplinary Forum on Subjective Well-Being*.

Liauw, I., Baelen, R. N., Borah, R. F., Yu, A. & Colby, A. 2018. Gratitude for teachers as a psychological resource for early adolescents: A mixed-methods study. *Journal of Moral Education*, 47, 397–414.

Lieberman, M. D., Eisenberger, N. I., Crockett, M. J., Tom, S. M., Pfeifer, J. H. & Way, B. M. 2007. Putting feelings into words: Affect labeling disrupts amygdala activity in response to affective stimuli. *Psychological Science (0956-7976)*, 18, 421–428.

Lin, W., Enright, R. & Klatt, J. 2013. A forgiveness intervention for Taiwanese young adults with insecure attachment. *Contemporary Family Therapy: An International Journal*, 35, 105–120.

Littman-Ovadia, H. & Steger, M. 2010. Character strengths and well-being among volunteers and employees: Toward an integrative model. *Journal of Positive Psychology*, 5, 419–430.

Lopez, S. J. 2013a. Making hope happen in the classroom. *Phi Delta Kappan*, 95, 19–22.

Lopez, S. J. 2013b. *Making hope happen: Create the future you want for yourself and others*, New York, NY, Atria Books.

Lyubomirsky, S. 2007. *The how of happiness: A scientific approach to getting the life you want*, New York, NY, Penguin Press.

Lyubomirsky, S., Sheldon, K. M. & Schkade, D. 2005. Pursuing happiness: The architecture of sustainable change. *Review of General Psychology*, 9, 111–131.

Lyubomirsky, S., Sousa, L. & Dickerhoof, R. 2006. The costs and benefits of writing, talking, and thinking about life's triumphs and defeats. *Journal of Personality and Social Psychology*, 90, 692–708.

Ma, L., Zhang, Y., Huang, C. & Cui, Z. 2020. Resilience-oriented cognitive behavioral interventions for depressive symptoms in children and adolescents: A meta-analytic review. *Journal of Affective Disorders*, 270, 150–164.

Maccann, C., Jiang, Y., Brown, L. E. R., Double, K. S., Bucich, M. & Minbashian, A. 2020. Emotional intelligence predicts academic performance: A meta-analysis. *Psychological Bulletin*, 146, 150–186.

Maher, A., Cobigo, V. & Stuart, H. 2013. Perspectives in rehabilitation: Conceptualizing belonging. *Disability and Rehabilitation*, 35, 1026–1032.

Marques, S., Lopez, S. & Pais-Ribeiro, J. 2011. 'Building hope for the future': A program to foster strengths in middle-school students. *Journal of Happiness Studies*, 12, 139–152.

Marques, S., Lopez, S. & Mitchell, J. 2013. The role of hope, spirituality and religious practice in adolescents' life satisfaction: longitudinal findings. *Journal of Happiness Studies*, 14, 251–261.

Marques, S. C., Lopez, S. J., Rose, S. & Robinson, C. 2014. Measuring and promoting hope in schoolchildren. In: Furlong, M. J., Gilman, R. & Huebner, E. S. (eds.), *Handbook of positive psychology in schools*, 2nd ed. New York, NY: Routledge/Taylor & Francis Group.

Martínez-Monteagudo, M. C., Inglés, C. J., Granados, L., Aparisi, D. & García-Fernández, J. M. 2019. Trait emotional intelligence profiles, burnout, anxiety, depression, and stress in secondary education teachers. *Personality and Individual Differences*, 142, 53–61.

Martins, A., Ramalho, N. & Morin, E. 2010. A comprehensive meta-analysis of the relationship between Emotional Intelligence and health. *Personality & Individual Differences*, 49, 554–564.

Mattingly, V. & Kraiger, K. 2019. Can emotional intelligence be trained? A meta-analytical investigation. *Human Resource Management Review*, 29, 140–155.

Mayer, J. D., Salovey, P., Caruso, D. R. & Sitarenios, G. 2003. Measuring emotional intelligence with the Msceit V20. *Emotion*, 3, 97–105.

Mccullough, M. E., Root, L. M. & Cohen, A. D. 2006. Writing about the benefits of an interpersonal transgression facilitates forgiveness. *Journal of Consulting and Clinical Psychology*, 74, 887–897.

Mcgonigal, K. 2016. *The Upside of Stress: Why Stress Is Good for You, and How to Get Good at It.* USA: Avery Publishing Group.

Mcgrath, H. & Noble, T. 2017. *Bounce Back! Years F-2*, Australia, Pearson Education Australia.

McGrath, R. E. 2015. Character strengths in 75 nations: An update. *The Journal of Positive Psychology*, 10, 41–52.

Mcmillan, T. E. 2005. Urban form and a child's trip to school: the current literature and a framework for future research. *Journal of Planning Literature*, 19, 440–456.

Medina, J. 2014. *Brain rules for baby: How to raise a smart and happy child from zero to five.*, Seatle, US, Pear Press.

Meter, D. J. & Card, N. A. 2016. Stability of children's and adolescents' friendships: A meta-analytic review. *Merrill-Palmer Quarterly*, 62, 252–284.

Mongrain, M., Chin, J. & Shapira, L. 2011. Practicing compassion increases happiness and self-esteem. *Journal of Happiness Studies*, 12, 963–981.

Morris, C., Simpson, J., Sampson, M. & Beesley, F. 2014. Cultivating positive emotions: A useful adjunct when working with people who self-harm? *Clinical Psychology & Psychotherapy*, 21, 352–362.

Moskowitz, J. T., Clark, M. S., Ong, A. D. & Gruber, J. 2014. The role of positive affect on thinking and decision-making: A tribute to Alice Isen. In: Gruber, J. & Moskowitz, J. T. (eds.), *Positive emotion: Integrating the light sides and dark sides.* New York, NY: Oxford University Press.

Moskowitz, J. T., Carrico, A. W., Duncan, L. G., Cohn, M. A., Cheung, E. O., Batchelder, A., Martinez, L., Segawa, E., Acree, M. & Folkman, S. 2017. Randomized controlled trial of a positive affect intervention for people newly diagnosed with HIV. *Journal of Consulting and Clinical Psychology*, 85, 409–423.

Myers, D. G. 1992. *The pursuit of happiness*, New York, Avon Books.

Myung-Sun, C. 2016. Relation Between lack of forgiveness and depression: The moderating effect of self-compassion. *Psychological Reports*, 119, 573–585.

Nakamura, J. & Csikszentmihalyi, M. 2005. Engagement in a profession: The case of undergraduate teaching. *Daedalus*, 134, 60–67.

Neff, K. 2020. *Self-compassion guided meditations and exercises* [Online]. Available: https://self-compassion.org/category/exercises/#exercises[Accessed].

Neff, K. D. 2003. The development and validation of a scale to measure self-compassion. *Self & Identity*, 2, 223.

Nelson, S. K., Layous, K., Cole, S. W. & Lyubomirsky, S. 2016. Do unto others or treat yourself? The effects of prosocial and self-focused behavior on psychological flourishing. *Emotion*, 16, 850–861.

Niemiec, R. M. 2018. *Character strengths interventions: A field guide for practitioners*, Boston, MA, Hogrefe Publishing.

Norem, J. K. 2001. *The positive power of negative thinking: Using defensive pessimism to manage anxiety and perform at your peak*, New York, NY, Basic Books.

Northern, J. R. & Lins-Dyer, M. T. 2003. Teachers' views of forgiveness for the resolution of conflicts between students in school. *Journal of Moral Education*, 32, 233.

Oppenheimer, M. F., Fialkov, C., Ecker, B. & Portnoy, S. 2014. Teaching to strengths: character education for urban middle school students. *Journal of Character Education*, 10, 91+.

Orth, U., Robins, R. W. & Soto, C. J. 2010. Tracking the trajectory of shame, guilt, and pride across the life span. *Journal of Personality & Social Psychology*, 99, 1061–1071.

Park, D., Yu, A., Metz, S. E., Tsukayama, E., Crum, A. J. & Duckworth, A. L. 2018. Beliefs about stress attenuate the relation among adverse life events, perceived distress, and self-control. *Child Development*, 89, 2059–2069.

Park, N. & Peterson, C. 2009. Strengths of character in schools. In: Gilman, R., Huebner, E. S. & Furlong, M. J. (eds.), *Handbook of positive psychology in schools.* New York, NY: Routledge/Taylor & Francis Group.

Pels, F., Kleinert, J. & Mennigen, F. 2018. Group flow: A scoping review of definitions, theoretical approaches, measures and findings. *PLoS ONE*, 13, 1–28.

Pennebaker, J. W. 1997. Writing about emotional experiences as a therapeutic process. *Psychological Science (0956-7976)*, 8, 162–166.

Pennebaker, J. W. 2018. Expressive writing in psychological science. *Perspectives on Psychological Science*, 13, 226–229.

Peterson, C. 2000. The future of optimism. *American Psychologist*, 55, 44–55.

Peterson, C. 2013. *Pursuing the good life: 100 reflections on positive psychology*, New York, NY, Oxford University Press.

Peterson, C. & Park, N. 2004. Classification and measurement of character strengths: implications for practice. In: Linley, P. A. & Joseph, S. (eds.), *Positive psychology in practice*. Hoboken, NJ: John Wiley & Sons Inc.

Peterson, C. & Seligman, M. E. P. 2004. *Character strengths and virtues: a handbook and classification*, New York, American Psychological Association; Oxford Univ Pr.

Pillay, N., Park, G., Kim, Y. K. & Lee, S. 2020. Thanks for your ideas: Gratitude and team creativity. *Organizational Behavior and Human Decision Processes*, 156, 69–81.

Proctor, C., Tsukayama, E., Wood, A. M., Maltby, J., Eades, J. F. & Linley, P. A. 2011. Strengths gym: The impact of a character strengths-based intervention on the life satisfaction and well-being of adolescents. *The Journal of Positive Psychology*, 6, 377–388.

Provine, R. R. 2000. The science of laughter. *Psychology Today*, 33, 58.

Puertas-Molero, P., Zurita-Ortega, F., Chacón-Cuberos, R., Castro-Sánchez, M., Ramírez-Granizo, I. & González-Valero, G. 2020. Emotional intelligence in the field of education: a meta-analysis. *La inteligencia emocional en el ámbito educativo: un meta-análisis.*, 36, 84–91.

Pullmer, R., Chung, J., Samson, L., Balanji, S. & Zaitsoff, S. 2019. A systematic review of the relation between self-compassion and depressive symptoms in adolescents. *Journal of Adolescence*, 74, 210–220.

Quinlan, D., Swain, N. & Vella-Brodrick, D. 2012. Character strengths interventions: building on what we know for improved outcomes. *Journal of Happiness Studies*, 13, 1145–1163.

Quinlan, D., Vella-Brodrick, D. A., Gray, A. & Swain, N. 2019. Teachers matter: Student outcomes following a strengths intervention are mediated by teacher strengths spotting. *Journal of Happiness Studies*, 20, 2507–2523.

Rashid, T. 2008. Positive psychotherapy. In: Lopez, S. J. (ed.), *Positive psychology: Exploring the best in people, Vol 4: Pursuing human flourishing.* Westport, CT: Praeger Publishers/Greenwood Publishing Group.

Rashid, T. & Seligman, M. 2019. *Positive psychotherapy workbook*, New York, Oxford University Press.

Reinhold, M., Bürkner, P. C. & Holling, H. 2018. Effects of expressive writing on depressive symptoms—A meta-analysis. *Clinical Psychology: Science & Practice*, 25, 1–1.

Reinke, W. M., Smith, T. E. & Herman, K. C. 2019. Family-school engagement across child and adolescent development. *School Psychology*, 34, 346–349.

Reivich, K. 2004. *Letting Go of Grudges. Assignment instructions for M. E. P. Seligman's Authentic Happiness Coaching Program.*

Reker, G. T. & Wong, P. T. P. 1988. Aging as an individual process: Toward a theory of personal meaning. In: Birren, J. E. & Bengtson, V. L. (eds.), *Emergent theories of aging*. New York, NY: Springer Publishing Co.

Resurrección, D. M., Salguero, J. M. & Ruiz-Aranda, D. 2014. Emotional intelligence and psychological maladjustment in adolescence: A systematic review. *Journal of Adolescence*, 37, 461–472.

Robertson, I. 2016. *The Stress Test: How Pressure Can Make You Stronger and Sharper*, London, Bloomsbury Publishing.

Roepke, A. M., Jayawickreme, E. & Riffle, O. M. 2014. Meaning and health: A systematic review. *Applied Research in Quality of Life*, 9, 1055–1079.

Ross, C. E. & Mirowsky, J. 1989. Explaining the social patterns of depression: control and problem solving—or support and talking? *Journal of Health & Social Behavior*, 30, 206–219.

Rotter, J. 1990. Internal versus external control of reinforcement: a case history of a variable. *American Psychologist*, 45, 489–493.

Ryan, R. M. & Deci, E. L. 2000. Self-determination theory and the facilitation of intrinsic motivation, social development, and well-being. *American Psychologist*, 55, 68–78.

Ryff, C. D. & Singer, B. 1998. The Contours of Positive Human Health. *Psychological Inquiry*, 9, 1.

Sallis, J. F., Conway, T. L., Prochaska, J. J., Mckenzie, T. L., Marshall, S. J. & Brown, M. 2001. The association of school environments with youth physical activity. *American Journal of Public Health*, 91, 618–620.

Salovey, P. & Mayer, J. D. 1990. Emotional intelligence. *Imagination, Cognition and Personality*, 9, 185–211.

Sánchez-Álvarez, N., Extremera, N. & Fernández-Berrocal, P. 2016. The relation between emotional intelligence and subjective well-being: A meta-analytic investigation. *Journal of Positive Psychology*, 11, 276–285.

Scheier, M. F. & Carver, C. S. 1987. Dispositional optimism and physical well-being: the influence of generalized outcome expectancies on health. *Journal of Personality*, 55, 169–210.

Schellenberg, B. J. I. & Gaudreau, P. 2020. Savoring and dampening with passion: How passionate people respond when good things happen. *Journal of Happiness Studies*, 21, 921–941.

Schmeichel, B. J., Vohs, K. D. & Baumeister, R. F. 2003. Intellectual performance and ego depletion: Role of the self in logical reasoning and other information processing. *Journal of Personality and Social Psychology*, 85, 33–46.

Schmidt, A., Neubauer, A. B., Dirk, J. & Schmiedek, F. 2020. The bright and the dark side of peer relationships: Differential effects of relatedness satisfaction and frustration at school on affective well-being in children's daily lives. *Developmental Psychology.*, 56: 1532–1546

Schrader, C. & Nett, U. 2018. The perception of control as a predictor of emotional trends during gameplay. *Learning and Instruction*, 54, 62–72.

Schutte, N. S., Malouff, J. M., Hall, L. E., Haggerty, D. J., Cooper, J. T., Golden, C. J. & Dornheim, L. 1998. Development and validation of a measure of emotional intelligence. *Personality and Individual Differences*, 25, 167–177.

Šebokova, G., Uhláriková, J. & Halamová, M. 2018. Cognitive and social sources of adolescent well-being: Mediating role of school belonging. *Studia Psychologica*, 60, 16–29.

Seligman, M. E. P. 1975. *Helplessness: On depression, development, and death*, New York, NY, W H Freeman/Times Books/ Henry Holt & Co.

Seligman, M. E. P. 1990. *Learned optimism: how to change your mind and your life*, New York, Alfred A Knopf.

Seligman, M. E. P. 2002. *Authentic happiness: using the new positive psychology to realize your potential for lasting fulfillment*, New York, Free Press.

Seligman, M. E. P. 2011. *Flourish: a visionary new understanding of happiness and well-being*, New York, Atria.

Seligman, M. E. P., Rashid, T. & Parks, A. C. 2006. Positive psychotherapy. *American Psychologist*, 61, 774–788.

Sharot, T. 2011. *The optimism bias: A tour of the irrationally positive brain*, New York, NY, Pantheon/Random House.

Shernoff, D. J. 2012. Engagement and positive youth development: Creating optimal learning environments. In: Harris, K. R., Graham, S., Urdan, T., Graham, S., Royer, J. M. & Zeidner, M. (eds.), *APA educational psychology handbook, Vol 2: Individual differences and cultural and contextual factors*. Washington, DC: American Psychological Association.

Shernoff, D. J. & Anderson, B. 2014. Interventions to create engagement and flow: Research and practice on optimal learning environments. In A. Parks (Ed.) *The Wiley-Blackwell handbook of positive psychology interventions*. USA: Wiley-Blackwell.

Shernoff, D. J., Csikszentmihalyi, M., Schneider, B. & Shernoff, E. S. 2003. Student engagement in high school classrooms from the perspective of flow theory. *School Psychology Quarterly*., 18: 158–176

Shoshani, A. & Russo-Netzer, P. 2017. Exploring and assessing meaning in life in elementary school children: Development and validation of the meaning in life in children questionnaire (Mil-CQ). *Personality and Individual Differences*, 104, 460–465.

Smith, T. E., Reinke, W. M., Herman, K. C. & Huang, F. 2019. Understanding family-school engagement across and within elementary- and middle-school contexts. *School Psychology*, 34, 363–375.

Snyder, C. R., Lopez, S. J., Shorey, H. S., Rand, K. L. & Feldman, D. B. 2003. Hope theory, measurements, and applications to school psychology. *School Psychology Quarterly*, 18, 122–139.

Snyder, C. R., Rand, K. L. & Sigmon, D. R. 2018. Hope theory: A member of the positive psychology family. In: Gallagher, M. W. & Lopez, S. J. (eds.), *The Oxford handbook of hope*. New York, NY: Oxford University Press.

Steger, M., Fitch-Martin, A., Donnelly, J. & Rickard, K. 2015. Meaning in life and health: proactive health orientation links meaning in life to health variables among american undergraduates. *Journal of Happiness Studies*, 16, 583–597.

Steger, M. F. 2012. Experiencing meaning in life: Optimal functioning at the nexus of well-being, psychopathology, and spirituality. In: Wong, P. T. P. (ed.), *The human quest for meaning: Theories, research, and applications*, 2nd ed. New York, NY: Routledge/Taylor & Francis Group.

Steger, M. F. 2017. Meaning in life and wellbeing. In: Slade, M., Oades, L. & Jarden, A. (eds.), *Wellbeing, recovery and mental health*. New York, NY: Cambridge University Press.

Steinberg, G. & Gano-Overway, L. A. 2003. Developing optimism skills to help youths overcome adversity. *JOPERD: The Journal of Physical Education, Recreation & Dance*, 74, 40.

Sterdt, E., Liersch, S. & Walter, U. 2014. Correlates of physical activity of children and adolescents: A systematic review of reviews. *Health Education Journal*, 73, 72–89.

Stratton, G. & Mullan, E. 2005. The effect of multicolor playground markings on children's physical activity level during recess. *Preventive Medicine: An International Journal Devoted to Practice and Theory*, 41, 828–833.

Street, H., Nathan, P., Durkin, K., Morling, J., Dzahari, M. A., Carson, J. & Durkin, E. 2004. Understanding the relationships between wellbeing, goal-setting and depression in children. *Australian and New Zealand Journal of Psychiatry*, 38, 155–161.

Stucke, T. S. & Baumeister, R. F. 2006. Ego depletion and aggressive behavior: Is the inhibition of aggression a limited resource? *European Journal of Social Psychology*, 36, 1–13.

Subkoviak, M. J., Enright, R. D., Wu, C.-R. & Gassin, E. A. 1995. Measuring interpersonal forgiveness in late adolescence and middle adulthood. *Journal of Adolescence*, 18, 641–655.

Tardy, C. M. & Snyder, B. 2004. 'That's why i do it': Flow and efl teachers' practices. *ELT Journal*, 58, 118–128.

Taylor, S. E. 1989. *Positive illusions: Creative self-deception and the healthy mind*, New York, NY, Basic Books.

Thompson, S. C. & Wierson, M. 2000. Enhancing perceived control in psychotherapy. In: Snyder, C. R. & Ingram, R. E. (eds.), *Handbook of psychological change: Psychotherapy processes & practices for the 21st century*. Hoboken, NJ: John Wiley & Sons Inc.

Tillman, K. S. & Prazak, M. 2018. Kids supporting kids: A 10–week small group curriculum for grief and loss in schools. *Counselling & Psychotherapy Research*, 18, 395–401.

Tong, E. W., Fredrickson, B., Chang, W. & Lim, Z. 2010. Re-examining hope: The roles of agency thinking and pathways thinking. *Cognition & Emotion*, 24, 1207–1215.

Tracy, J. L. & Robins, R. W. 2004. Putting the self into self-conscious emotions: A theoretical model. *Psychological Inquiry*, 15, 103–125.

Tracy, J. L. & Robins, R. W. 2007. The psychological structure of pride: A tale of two facets. *Journal of Personality and Social Psychology*, 92, 506–525.

Travagin, G., Margola, D. & Revenson, T. A. 2015. How effective are expressive writing interventions for adolescents? A meta-analytic review. *Clinical Psychology Review*, 36, 42–55.

Trinder, H. & Salkovskis, P. M. 1994. Personally relevant intrusions outside the laboratory: Longterm suppression increases intrusion. *Behaviour Research and Therapy*, 32, 833–842.

Tse, D. C. K., Lau, V. W.-Y., Perlman, R. & Mclaughlin, M. 2020a. The development and validation of the autotelic personality questionnaire. *Journal of Personality Assessment*, 102, 88–101.

Tse, D. C. K., Nakamura, J. & Csikszentmihalyi, M. 2020b. Living well by 'flowing' well: The indirect effect of autotelic personality on well-being through flow experience. *The Journal of Positive Psychology*.

Tugade, M. M. & Fredrickson, B. L. 2004. Resilient individuals use positive emotions to bounce back from negative emotional experiences. *Journal of Personality and Social Psychology*, 86, 320–333.

Vaillant, G. E. 2003. *Aging well: surprising guideposts to a happier life*, New York, Little, Brown.

Vallerand, R. J. & Houlfort, N. 2003. Passion at work: Toward a new conceptualization. In: Skarlicki, D., Gilliand, S. & Steiner, D. (eds.), *Research in Social Issues in Management*. Greenwich, CT: Information Age Publishing Inc.

Vallerand, R. J., Salvy, S.-J., Mageau, G. A., Elliot, A. J., Denis, P. L., Grouzet, F. M. E. & Blanchard, C. 2007. On the role of passion in performance. *Journal of Personality*, 75, 505–533.

Van Cappellen, P., Rice, E. L., Catalino, L. I. & Fredrickson, B. L. 2018. Positive affective processes underlie positive health behaviour change. *Psychology & Health*, 33, 77–97.

Van Reken, R. E. & Pollock, D. C. 1999. *The third culture kid experience: growing up among worlds*, Yarmouth, ME, Intercultural Pr.

Vanitha, B. & Husain, A. 2011. Daily hassles among school teachers. *Journal of the Indian Academy of Applied Psychology*, 37, 240–245.

Vanoyen Witvliet, C., Ludwig, T. E. & Vander Laan, K. L. 2001. Granting forgiveness or harboring grudges: implications for emotion, physiology, and health. *Psychological Science* 12, (0956–7976).

Von Culin, K. R., Tsukayama, E. & Duckworth, A. L. 2014. Unpacking grit: Motivational correlates of perseverance and passion for long-term goals. *The Journal of Positive Psychology*, 9, 306–312.

Wang, Y., Wang, X., Yang, J., Zeng, P. & Lei, L. 2020. Body talk on social networking sites, body surveillance, and body shame among young adults: The roles of self-compassion and gender. *Sex Roles: A Journal of Research*, 82, 731–742.

Waters, L. & Stokes, H. 2015. Positive education for school leaders: Exploring the effects of emotion-gratitude and action-gratitude. *The Australian Educational and Developmental Psychologist*, 32, 1–22.

Watkins, P. C., Woodward, K., Stone, T. & Kolts, R. L. 2003. Gratitude and happiness: development of a measure of gratitude, and relationships with subjective well-being. *Social Behavior & Personality: an international journal*, 31, 431–452.

Watson, D., Clark, L. A. & Tellegen, A. 1988. Development and validation of brief measures of positive and negative affect: the Panas scales. *Journal of Personality & Social Psychology*, 54, 1063–1070.

Wegner, D. M. 2011. When you put things out of mind, where do they go? In: Gernsbacher, M. A., Pew, R. W., Hough, L. M. & Pomerantz, J. R. (eds.), *Psychology and the real world: Essays illustrating fundamental contributions to society*. New York, NY: Worth Publishers.

Werner, E. E. 1993. Risk, resilience, and recovery: Perspectives from the Kauai Longitudinal Study. *Development and Psychopathology*, 5, 503–515.

WHO, W. H. O. 2020. *Prevalence of insufficient physical activity*. [Online]. Available: https://www.who.int/gho/ncd/risk_factors/physical_activity_text/en/ [Accessed].

Williams, P. 2011. Pathways to positive education at geelong grammar school integrating positive psychology and appreciative inquiry. *AI Practitioner*, 13, 8–13.

Wingspread 2004. Wingspread declaration on school connections. *Journal of School Health*, 74, 233–234.

Wise, D. & Rosqvist, J. 2006. Explanatory style and well-being. In: Thomas, J. C., Segal, D. L. & Hersen, M. (eds.), *Comprehensive Handbook of Personality and Psychopathology, Vol. 1: Personality and Everyday Functioning.* Hoboken, NJ: John Wiley & Sons, Inc.

Wong, P. T. P. 2011. Positive psychology 20: Towards a balanced interactive model of the good life. *Canadian Psychology/Psychologie canadienne*, 52, 69–81.

Wood, A. M., Froh, J. J. & Geraghty, A. W. A. 2010. Gratitude and well-being: A review and theoretical integration. *Clinical Psychology Review*, 30, 890–905.

Woods, P. A. 2016. Authority, power and distributed leadership. *Management in Education*, 30, 155–160.

Worthington, E. L., JR. 2006. *Forgiveness and reconciliation: Theory and application*, New York, NY, Routledge/Taylor & Francis Group.

Worthington, E. L. 2013. *Moving forward: six steps to forgiving yourself and breaking free from the past*, Colorado Springs, Colo, Water Brook.

Worthington, E. L., JR., Kurusu, T. A., Collins, W., Berry, J. W., Ripley, J. S. & Baier, S. N. 2000. Forgiving usually takes time: A lesson learned by studying interventions to promote forgiveness. *Journal of Psychology and Theology*, 28, 3–20.

Xu, Z., Huang, F., Kösters, M., Staiger, T., Becker, T., Thornicroft, G. & Rüsch, N. 2018. Effectiveness of interventions to promote help-seeking for mental health problems: systematic review and meta-analysis. *Psychological Medicine*, 48, 2658–2667.

CHAPTER

The mechanisms that enable successful wellbeing interventions

For years, wellbeing and happiness seemed unattainable, unmalleable and irrelevant. Many psychologists did not believe it was possible to alter our levels of wellbeing; therefore, very little work was carried out to prove otherwise. The first cohort of researchers that ignored the majority and developed pioneering wellbeing programmes in late 1970s and early 1980s were Fordyce (1983), Fordyce (1977) and Lichter (1980). They encouraged participants to spend more time socialising, keep busy, become present-oriented. They tried to see if applying a range of activities would have any effect on individual levels of wellbeing and they found noticeable and long-lasting effects. Following on from their studies, the second cohort of researchers tried to explore the individual interventions that may be included in a programme to identify which intervention was more effective. This resulted in an avalanche of studies, some of which were presented in the previous chapter. However, since very little is known about the mechanisms through which positive psychology interventions work (Schueller and Parks, 2014), the third wave of research in wellbeing interventions attempted to figure out how these interventions work and in what conditions, so that we can design the most effective wellbeing initiatives in schools and beyond. Before we delve into what works, let us briefly review what does not work when designing a wellbeing programme or an intervention.

Beware of wellbeing

Not for all

Over a decade ago, when in London, I attended a guest lecture about epigenetics. The speaker, Michael Pluess, introduced us to the latest research, and as he guided us eloquently through the difficult terminology, even though there were over a hundred people in the room, it was so quiet that we could hear birds singing outside the auditorium. When he finished, we all sat there dumbfounded for a few seconds until someone raised their hand and asked: *Why do people not know about your research?*, to which Pluess responded: *It's too complicated for the media to get.*

The research he spoke about was a pioneering perspective on individual differences among people. Researchers found that in the same way that we have brain plasticity, we may also have a predisposition to a genetic plasticity (Belsky et al., 2009). What it means is that despite all of us having similar life experiences, the way we react to our experiences is different. This is due to us being at a different point of the spectrum in genetic environmental sensitivity (Pluess et al., 2018). Children and adults who are highly sensitive to their environment are more susceptible to significant changes of their thoughts, feelings and behaviours due to the impact of the environment in which they live. Often, when they are sensitive to the negative situations, they are also sensitive to the positive interventions, giving them a greater capacity for growth (Kennedy, 2013). This predisposition is also highly heritable (Greven et al., 2019). This finding has a significant implication for the school community and the wellbeing strategy. It explains why some of us gain much more from wellbeing interventions than others. In a study with over 2,000 children, the researchers found that boys with higher sensitivity to their environment benefited more from an antibullying intervention than those who scored low in the sensitivity to their environment (Nocentini et al., 2018). Similarly, when a wellbeing programme was introduced to a group of 11-year-old girls at risk, overall, the girls benefitted from it for up to 6 months, but a year later, their average level of depression had returned to the pre-intervention state (Pluess and Boniwell, 2015). The only exception to this were the 30% of the girls who scored the highest on the environmental sensitivity scale. Their reduction in depression persisted 12 months after the wellbeing programme concluded, meaning that they gained immensely from this intervention.

These individual differences need to be considered when implementing a wellbeing strategy in schools. Not all interventions will have a lasting impact on children, and not all children will benefit from a wellbeing intervention long term. Some will need to re-engage more frequently with wellbeing interventions than others. However, another important point to consider is that children are not the only ones who can benefit from wellbeing initiatives like this. High sensitivity to environment continues into adulthood, challenging the myth that it is difficult for adults to change their old ways (Lionetti et al., 2018). In fact, not only is it not as difficult, but for some individuals it may be relatively easy to make long-lasting changes, regardless if they are young or older.

Be careful what you wish for

Happiness is an important aspect of wellbeing. When people are happy, they experience higher levels of positive emotions, lower levels of negative emotions and are more satisfied with their lives (Diener et al., 1999). All that most parents want for their children is usually to be happy (Seligman, 2002). Happiness is the most endorsed goal in western society, which has grown to value it immensely (Myers, 2000). We publish books about the pursuit of happiness, encourage people to put themselves first and create plans to become happier. As part of wellbeing programmes in schools, we teach children ways in which they can boost their happiness and wellbeing. Yet, even though we focus so much on it, our levels of depression and anxiety have not decreased significantly. So what are we doing wrong, and how can we avoid doing it when designing a wellbeing strategy in schools?

Growing research suggests that seeking out happiness can make us unhappy (Mauss et al., 2011) and cause us to experience higher levels of depression (Ford et al., 2014), which may be one of the reasons why attending wellbeing programmes and doing interventions doesn't work so well for some of us. This is also true for young people, many of whom are so focussed on being happy that they become worried about happiness and losing it while they are in the middle of experiencing it (Gentzler et al., 2019). When in a positive situation (e.g., getting a top grade or spending time with friends), people who value happiness experience lower levels of psychological wellbeing, subjective wellbeing and are less satisfied with their lives. They also reported more symptoms of depression, which is ironic, given that happiness is so important to them. It is as if valuing happiness made them compare their idealised vision of what it should feel like to get a top grade or hang out with their friends, and when they compared it to the actual feeling, they were dissatisfied.

Imagine you are walking into a room and someone sits you down comfortably and asks you *"try and make yourself feel as happy as possible"* while you are listening to classical music (Stravinsky). Would you be able to think happy thoughts and make yourself happy on demand? If yes, you are a minority group, as most people in this situation feel more miserable than if they were simply asked to listen to music, which would possibly enhance their positive emotions anyway (Schooler et al., 2003). This puts into perspective some of the things we say to others when they don't look happy: *cheer up, think happy thoughts, it will be alright.* Unbeknownst to us, we may be making them more miserable by trying to cheer them up.

In addition to making them less happy, some researchers warn that the pursuit of happiness can make us more lonely (Mauss et al., 2012). It may be because when we start putting ourselves first, we become more self-focussed and we lose the sight of the important people in our lives (Nelson et al., 2016). This is how paradoxically wanting to be happy makes us drift away from the source of our happiness, which is other people, making us feel more lonely. Research is clear that being other-people focussed makes us happier than being focussed on ourselves (Ko et al., 2019). These are just some of the points that need to be considered when designing a wellbeing strategy.

As with everything in life, there is a caveat in all this, which relates to our culture (Ford et al., 2015). In an individualistic culture, such as the western world, the pursuit of happiness is often associated with focussing on self, whereas in a collectivist culture, such as in Asia, the pursuit of happiness means that we seek out social engagement by enhancing connectedness with our friends, colleagues or new people in our lives. Given that social connection is associated with heightened levels of wellbeing, saying to someone *"think happy thoughts,"* may in fact redirect them to a social-connection path, which may result in being happier after all.

This is why when designing a wellbeing strategy for school, it is better to refocus everyone's goals to bringing the school community together or getting together to create something special for others, rather than setting up a goal to be happier or well. Otherwise, that self-obsession and self-focus of becoming better may lead some people astray, and rather than helping students and teachers lead happier lives, we may inadvertently cause their unhappiness, loneliness and misery.

Prescriptive wellbeing

One of my students created a wellbeing programme, which was based on the research suggesting that the happiest people experience five positive emotions to one negative (Fredrickson and Losada, 2005). This is a theory created by Losada's Non-linear Dynamic Model that was subsequently disputed (Fredrickson and Losada, 2013, Brown et al., 2013). However, what my student told his class was that they need to make sure that every time they feel sad, they think of five things that make them happy. This oversimplification of the theory worked for some, but for others, it seemed like a stressful thing to do. Imagine going through some hardship and frantically finding ways to experience not one or two, but five positive emotions. Does it mean that we have to experience one event with a variety of positive emotions, or five different events that would give us a predominant positive emotion? Regardless of what option we go for, it seems like a lot of hard work; therefore, this approach to enhancing wellbeing is not sustainable. Being too prescriptive does not work for many people.

Another issue with prescriptive wellbeing is that we ignore individual differences. For example, research on optimism shows us that optimistic thinking is beneficial for us (Segerstrom, 2009). However, research about defensive pessimism suggests that there are some people who need to think pessimistically and tap into the worst-case scenario; if they are not allowed to do so, and keep focussing on the best-case scenario, they become even more anxious about their future event (Norem, 2001). In other words, defensive pessimism is a strategy of getting the best out of anxieties we can. While it works for some, it might not work for others. This is why it is crucial to ensure that we consider each individual student and their preferences before we ask all students to practise optimism or any other activities.

When we use prescriptive measures for teaching wellbeing, what we are doing is sharing scientific knowledge and assuming that people will know what is right for them, so they will simply take it on board. However, human beings are complex creatures. We might know what is good for us, but it does not mean that we will do it. There are so many other factors to consider. One such factor is our ability to self-regulate and control our urges, which may not serve us well (Baumeister and Vohs, 2007). Other factors are down to us simply not agreeing with the researchers' views, so we don't see a reason as to why we should comply. Yet, another reason is our motivation to do it (Ryan and Deci, 2000). Sharing knowledge and making it relevant to individuals are two different things. This is why knowledge of wellbeing may help, but helping the school community assimilate their knowledge is a more powerful way to enhance their wellbeing.

Mind you, this type of approach might work well for some. Moreover, they may in fact request it. I have a friend who lives her life that way. She is incredibly self-disciplined and if she believes something is right for her she simply does it. One day a few years ago, she was going through a hard time. She felt low and decided she was going to do something about it. With this in mind, she arranged to meet with me and asked: *what type of changes would a person need to introduce to boost their happiness?* I laughed when I heard her say that thinking she was joking, but she couldn't be more serious. I suggested we could have a chat about what has worked for her in the past and how she can build on it, but she had no time for coaching. All she wanted to know was the science. I gave her five evidence-based wellbeing interventions, which she dutifully wrote down in her diary and then, to my surprise, she contacted me two months later to thank me as she felt considerably better after doing them every day for the last eight weeks. This prescriptive approach has worked for her, but it is just not something I would recommend for most people.

Stigmatising negativity

In our society it is "cool" to be happy. When a child feels sad, angry or lonely, we put a spotlight on them and try to help them, fuss around asking why they feel so sad and try to turn their negative emotions into positive. When doing so, we are also communicating a very important message to them: we don't like to see you sad, angry or lonely, we prefer to see you happy.

Our behaviour, although well intentioned, may be actually damaging to the child. It makes experiencing negativity maladaptive and unwanted. Instead of stigmatising negativity, the message we should be sending to students is that feeling bad is human, it is normal and we should not feel bad about it. Consequently, it is ok to leave a child feeling sad for a period of time and give them space to experience these emotions. It is ok to allow students to feel angry. It is ok to allow them to feel lonely and spend a school break on their own, if they choose to do so. Without allowing ourselves to experience these emotions we are unable to come up with strategies to process them, which are important life-skills to learn.

Each one of these negative emotions serves an important purpose for us. Sadness alerts us that something important is missing from our lives, be it a mammy, a cuddle or feeling safe. Anger cautions us that someone was unfairly treated. Loneliness notifies us that in this specific environment we feel unwanted, insignificant or insecure. All these are important message that our body sends us to process, so that we can make changes in our lives. When we desperately try to avoid them and focus on turning them around too quickly into positive emotions, we will become deaf to them in the future, while they will continue to bubble up under the surface. This is why stigmatising negativity is not a useful tool for keeping our wellbeing in check. In fact, it does the opposite, makes us even more miserable.

Demonising negative feelings and telling students what emotions they should ideally feel can easily backfire. Unfortunately, sometimes we create an expectation of students that they need to feel certain emotions and behave in a certain way, because society wants them to do so or because it is better for them. The social pressure associated with feeling happy can be particularly harmful to us. The more social pressure we are put under not to feel sad or anxious, the more depressive symptoms we usually tend to develop (Dejonckheere and Bastian, 2020). Similarly, when we overemphasise the importance of positive emotions and try desperately to avoid feeling negative, we may start to ruminate more (McGuirk et al., 2018). Our negative thoughts and feelings need to be expressed to help us feel better (Lyubomirsky et al., 2006). Keeping them buried in our heads makes things worse. Stigmatising negativity may get in the way of this useful process, which is why it should be avoided.

In western societies, happiness and positive emotions are often significantly valued. At the same time, the experiences of negativity are not only unwanted but also not valued. When we don't see the benefit of negative emotions, we may be more inclined to suppress them. This attitude not only affects our physical health (Luong et al., 2016) but could also have a significant impact on our ability to self-control.

Inspired by Fyodor Dostoyewski's "Winter notes on summer impressions" (1863), an experiment was carried out asking participants not to think of a polar bear for a period of time (Wegner, 2011). Suppressing thoughts resulted in participants not only thinking about the polar bears more, but the thought of it kept popping up spontaneously in their heads regularly for a few days. They had never thought about polar bears before, yet after suppressing the thoughts for a few minutes, the image became imprinted on their minds. The effect is even more significant when the thoughts we are suppressing are personally relevant (Trinder and Salkovskis, 1994), which is why any form of suppression needs to be replaced with either expression through writing or talking.

This is also why it is crucial not to demonise negativity, not to stigmatise it to an extent where students would be asked to keep thinking positively. This suppression of negativity could be more damaging to them than learning wellbeing skills. Students need to learn to live with whatever is on their mind and perhaps come up with some techniques for releasing it rather than pretending it does not exist.

Wellbeing strategy

An analysis of a large number of health-promotion programmes found that developing a framework prior to creating a strategy was a great foundation for success (Hung et al., 2014). This may be a framework deriving from one of the theories of wellbeing, such as PERMA (Seligman, 2011). Alternatively, it may be a framework offered by one of the trusted national or international organisations, such as UNICEF or WHO, or a school deciding to create their own framework that best reflects their students' needs, which may be an amalgamation of various models of wellbeing. Regardless of what framework is selected, it will allow the whole school to understand what they are working towards and what action everyone needs to take to enhance their wellbeing.

The second component that improves the effectiveness of a wellbeing strategy is the support and commitment of the school community stakeholders, such as staff, board management, government, health agencies and others (Hung et al., 2014). Without the stakeholder support, all parties will meander in different directions without fully engaging in the process. A study that a colleague and I carried out shortly after the COVID-19-related school closure showed that the involvement of all staff in a difficult decision about what schools should do to sustain the continuity of learning made them more likely to firm up an arrangement for teachers to contact pupils regularly (Burke & Dempsey, 2020). The involvement of other parties not only motivates us to action but also provides higher chances for commitment to change. They need to be an integral part of the wellbeing strategy from the beginning, so that they have their say throughout the process.

The third enabler for implementing a successful wellbeing strategy is adopting a multidisciplinary approach (Hung et al., 2014). The majority of the wellbeing programmes in schools are psycho-social (O'Toole, 2017), yet, there are many other approaches to wellbeing. For example, a *Lego Serious Play* for older pupils and adults offers a play-approach to enhancing wellbeing (Tseng, 2017). Eliciting students' voice and identifying their perception of wellbeing is yet another approach that could be taken with children from an early age (Roffey, 2015). Helping students practise mindful reflection (Ahmed and Schwind, 2018) or discuss some of the philosophers and their teachings in relation to wellbeing (Mortari and Ubbiali, 2017) may also prove helpful. These and similar multidisciplinary approaches should be considered when designing a wellbeing strategy for schools.

Some of the most effective ways of implementing sustainable wellbeing change in schools come from an integration of researchers' and policymakers' perspective, with participant groups, that is, parents and children, providing their own perspectives, as well as teachers' full involvement in offering suggestions for a change (Rütten et al., 2019). This is why, using the research from this book (researchers' view), combined with a framework created by the department/ministry for education in your country (policy-maker's view) and discussing it with a wellbeing committee (participants' view) that combines all levels of the school community, is the best way to improve the chances of a wellbeing strategy being successful.

What usually does not work well is being reactive to the problems in school. Introducing an anti-bullying programme and a wellbeing intervention after a serious bullying incident has happened is less effective than designing a preventative strategy that tackles various issues systematically before they happen (Barry et al., 2013). A once-off intervention may tick a box in relation to doing "something" to boost students' wellbeing in your school, but the effect will be more significant if a multicomponent school initiative was implemented instead (Shepherd et al., 2002). Sadly, most of the evidence-based wellbeing interventions and programmes are short-term, but it is the long-term strategy filled with varied activities for the school community that will make most impact in your school (Svane et al., 2019). It will set your school up for success, prevent many issues from happening and allow you to be more in control of your community's wellbeing.

Free choice

In order for any wellbeing intervention or programme in our schools to work, we need to ensure that students have a choice of what they practice. Human beings aim to be self-governed, we want to initiate our own actions, cause our own incidents and act in our own volition (Wehmeyer et al., 2017). Imposing any wellbeing-related actions on the school community may result in them developing an extrinsic motivation, which is not the optimal place to be in order to enhance their wellbeing. The famous saying: "you can bring a horse to water, but you can't make him drink it" is a very true depiction of the reason that intrinsic motivation is so important.

Intrinsic motivation means that we do something because we want to, not because someone promised us anything, forced us to do it, or because it would be a good thing to do, instead, we engage in the wellbeing activities in school because we choose to do so (Ryan and Deci, 2000). When we engage in intrinsically motivated activities, we feel more authentic and self-fulfilled. Only then, a significant change can happen.

Recently, I chatted with a group of students who had been introduced to mindfulness. I asked them how they got on and all of them looked at each other and made faces. They said they *had to* do it, as everyone in their class had to attend the 8-week course. As I listened to them complain about it, my heart was melting. I thought that the school was missing something very important. Through their well-intended strategy, they created an extrinsic motivation in students without recognising that they should be the ones to choose what interventions they use. We are different and different interventions work for us. Forcing mindfulness on the school community, without them making a choice to do it, will not only have a negative effect on them, but may also deter them from using that wellbeing resource in the future. Some of the activities are an acquired taste.

Last year, I co-organised a wellbeing event at our university, the aim of which was to showcase our team's research and share good practice. We invited a few schools to present what they have been doing to boost their community's wellbeing. One school stood out, as they had shown a 7-min animoto (video) of all the interventions they had introduced for students to choose from. They ranged from activities such as gratitude, savouring, acts of kindness through to writing about their best possible selves, gardening and a healthy-body week project. Then, two students stood up and shared what had worked the best for them. The interesting thing was that both mentioned different activities and shared a joke on the stage about how one of them would not like to do an activity that was the other student's favourite. It was a great way to show the importance of free choice when selecting wellbeing interventions, only then they can have a powerful impact on the school community.

While there is some research that does not consider self-selection an important element of a wellbeing intervention (Silberman, 2007), a review of over 50 studies found that self-selection had an overall positive impact on the participants' outcomes, whereby those who have self-selected activities had a more significant chance of enhancing their wellbeing and reducing their depression than those who have been assigned to an activity (Sin and Lyubomirsky, 2009). With this in mind a person-activity fit diagnostic tool was created to help people self-select from a range of positive psychology activities (Lyubomirsky, 2007). The activities include expressing gratitude, cultivating optimism, avoiding overthinking and social comparison, practising acts of kindness, nurturing relationships, developing strategies for coping, learning to forgive, doing more activities that truly engage you, savouring life's joys, committing to your goals, practising religion and spirituality, taking care of your body. Table 4.1 provides the details of each category of activities. When assessing how suitable each wellbeing activity is to you, you rate it from 1 to 7 using each of the following: natural (feels authentic), enjoy (find it interesting and challenging), value (identify with it and value it), guilty (forcing self as I feel guilty not doing it) and situation (my circumstances, situations I find myself in compel me to do it, or someone else wants me to do it). The best activities are those with the highest score measured as an average of *natural, enjoy* and *value*, minus an average *of guilty* and *situation*. This questionnaire is simple, and provides individuals with a score for each one of the mentioned activities, thus allowing us to identify, which activity is the best for us.

We may help the school community select activities from the selection of groups, for example, committing to goals or taking care of our body. Alternatively, each category of activities may represent a week, or a month and students are asked to select from various interventions that address taking care of your body. This way they will be exposed to many different activities by the end of the year and may be able to make a more informed decision as to what they like.

At this point, it is important to note that there are limits to the choices we offer students. Too much choice can cause anxiety and indecision (Schwartz, 2004). If they have ten interventions to choose this week, chances are they will not do well

TABLE 4.1 Positive Psychology Interventions recommended in the person-fit diagnostic tool, adapted from Lyubomirsky, 2007

Intervention category	Example of an intervention
Expressing gratitude	Counting your blessings from what you have through contemplation or diary-writing, conveying your gratitude and appreciation to one or more individuals whom you've never properly thanked.
Cultivating optimism	Keeping a journal in which you imagine and write about the best possible future for yourself or practise looking at the bright side of every situation.
Avoiding overthinking and social comparison	Using strategies, such as distraction to cut down on how often you dwell on your problems and compare yourself to others
Practising acts of kindness	Doing good thing for others, either directly or anonymously, either spontaneously or planned.
Nurturing relationships	Picking a relationship in need of strengthening and investing time and energy in healing, cultivating, affirming and enjoying it.
Developing strategies for coping	Practising ways to endure or surmount a recent stress, hardship or trauma
Learning to forgive	Keeping a journal or writing a letter in which you work on letting go of anger and resentment towards one or more individuals who have hurt or wronged you.
Doing more activities that truly engage you	Increasing the number of experiences at home and work in which you "lose" yourself because they are challenging and absorbing
Savouring life's joys	Paying close attention, taking delight and replaying life's momentary pleasures and wonders through thinking, writing, drawing or sharing with others
Committing to your goals	Picking one, two or three significant goals that are meaningful to you and devoting time and effort to pursuing them.
Practising religion or spirituality	Becoming more involved in your church, temple or mosque, or reading and pondering spiritually themed books
Taking care of your body	Engaging in physical activity, meditating, smiling and laughing

practising any of them. Instead if you offer them two interventions to choose from this week, for example, mindful meditation vs mindful running, or practising gratitude vs savouring, or practising spirituality vs learning to forgive, they will be more likely to try at least one of them out. Choices are particularly challenging for maximisers, who are searching for perfection in their decision (Schwartz et al., 2002). The more choice is offered to them, the more regret they have for not selecting other options and the worse it makes them feel. This is yet another reason why when creating a wellbeing strategy for your school community offer people a free choice to choose their intervention but limit it to two or three choices.

While the self-selection aspect of applying wellbeing activities appears in many research findings, there is no direct evidence to suggest that self-selection enhance wellbeing. There is, however, evidence that when we self-select, we are more likely to engage with an activity and adhere to it (Schueller, 2010). Higher levels of engagement with an activity increase our intrinsic motivation and the chances of the activities positively influencing our wellbeing. This may be the mechanism through which the efficacy of wellbeing interventions work.

Another model of self-selection of activities allows individuals to self-select from a range of intervention relating to an acronym ACTIONS (Boniwell, 2017). A stands for Active interventions that include physical activity and sport; C stands for Calming Interventions which include mindfulness and meditation; T stands for Thinking or Taking Stick which is about learning from and integrating positive and negative past in a present situation; I stands for Identity-related actions that delve into personal strengths and self-identity; O stands for Optimisation that helps individuals with goal setting, focuses them on the future and an improvement of their current circumstances; N describes actions to do with self-soothing, taking care of self and pleasure-seeking behaviours; and S refers to Social actions to do with building and maintaining positive relationships. There is no questionnaire assessing participants interest in any of the interventions; however, students, teachers and others may select a category of interventions that appeals to them most. Table 4.2 provides examples of such interventions (Boniwell and Tunariu, 2019).

It is important that whatever programme, initiatives or single interventions are introduced in your school to enhance their wellbeing, they are done with dignity and free choice. It is good for students to try them and it is good to encourage them to share some of the benefits of the activities. However, which activity they want to continue with is ultimately up to them.

TABLE 4.2 Positive Psychology Interventions clustered using the ACTIONS acronym, adapted from Boniwell and Tunariu, 2019

Intervention category	Example of an intervention
Active	Aerobic exercise, dance, tai chi, walking together, yoga, health check
Calming	Mindful breathing, mindful body scan, mindful listening, mindful non-judging, mindful observation, loving kindness meditation, mindful acceptance, the serenity prayer
Thinking	Discussing beliefs, your worst life experience, benefit-finding, one door closes, another opens, positive reminiscence, your best ever life experience, three good things, capturing happiness, three funny things, life review
Identity	Positive introduction, strengths identification, using strengths in a new way, identity groups, best possible self, job crafting
Optimising	Mental time travel, your life course journal, positive bibliography, positive statements, optimism, resilience, psychological capital, hope quest, goal setting, coaching, the miracle question, obituary, good enough, bar at the right height
Nourishing	Massage, self-compassion meditation, cultivating sacred moments, savouring, rest-breaks at work, nourishing happiness, me time
Social	Socialising, family strengths tree, strengths date, grateful thoughts, forgiveness, kindness day, counting kindness, active communication, compassionate action, active-constructive responding, gratitude visit, gift of time

Another way to consider when deciding on which intervention to self-select is by viewing the interventions from the perspective of time. Some relate to the past, for example, when students are asked to reflect on what they have done in the past that made them happy; others relate to the present, for example, when students are asked how they use character strengths every day; alternatively, they may relate to the future, for example, when students are asked about their hopes about what is going to happen in the future. Therefore, all interventions that are being carried out in wellbeing programmes in schools fall into one of the three categories. The question is which time perspective is optimal for wellbeing?

A review of various studies have found that interventions that relate to the present or future time perspective are significantly more effective than those that help us tap into the past (Wellenzohn et al., 2016). Table 4.3 provides an example of activities that are set in the past, present and future (Boniwell et al., 2014) that can be used in a wellbeing programme.

Please note that even though present- and future-oriented activities seemed to have shown higher levels of wellbeing increase, it does not mean that we should disregard the past-oriented activities. Balanced time perspective, whereby their thoughts are directed towards the past, present and future, throughout the day are the optimal state of mind (Boniwell and Zimbardo, 2004). Predominant focus on one of the perspectives results in imbalance. For instance, people experiencing post-traumatic stress disorder direct a lot of their thoughts every day towards their negative past (Zimbardo et al., 2012). Also, students who are focussed predominantly on future are more successful academically, but less likely to enjoy their lives than those who have a balanced perspective, whereby they might take time out from their ambitions and enjoy the here and now (Zimbardo and Boyd, 2008). Therefore, time-orientation balance is required when promoting wellbeing interventions in your school.

TABLE 4.3 Time-oriented wellbeing interventions, adapted from Boniwell et al., 2014

Time perspective	Wellbeing interventions
Past	Expressive writing
	Forgiveness letter
	Positive portfolio
	Positive reminiscence
	"What went well" exercise
	Involvement in community projects/events
	Birthdays calendar
	Questions reflecting on regret
Present	Reducing passive activities, e.g., tv watching
	Enhancing meaningfulness
	Savouring
	Mindfulness
	Playlist
Future	Future best possible self
	Funeral service/epitaph
	Worry reduction
	Self-regulation activities

Dosage, variety & support

Whether or not an intervention is effective depends on their dosage, variety, sequence and social support (Lyubomirsky and Layous, 2013). Let's look at dosage first. Dosage refers to the frequency of engaging with an intervention. For example, you may be introducing students to an intervention and then asking them to practise it at home. Initially, they may find the activity interesting and do it every day, but after a while they may be bored with it as the activity will no longer offer them a challenge. You forcing them to do it daily may be counterproductive. Those who consider the activity important or meaningful tend to do it several times a week or everyday (Parks et al., 2012). When they don't value it, they do not engage with it as frequently. This is why when creating a wellbeing strategy, it is crucial to think of ways in which students can find the activities meaningful. Usually, discussing why we do these activities and offering examples that are relevant to students make these activities more meaningful to them.

At the same time, we need to be balanced in our approach. Overdoing an activity might not be good for us. For example, mindfulness is useful, but it follows an inverted u-shaped trajectory whereby too much mindfulness may no longer be as beneficial as a moderate amount of it (Willoughby and Tosey, 2007, Britton, 2019). Just because someone practises something every day, it does not necessarily make them feel better. Sometimes doing a few activities on 1 day a week makes them more effective than spreading them over a week (Lyubomirsky et al., 2005). It is as if we are getting a wellbeing booster shot that keeps us going for a few days or weeks. However, all this depends on the individuals and their lifestyle. Some are interested in doing activities a few times a week, others every day or weekly. It is good for everyone to decide this for themselves.

What matters more is their long-term engagement with the activities rather than how often they are doing them. For example, those who counted their blessing once a week for 6 weeks saw more gains in wellbeing than those who did it three times a week (Lyubomirsky et al., 2005). Longer engagement with interventions shows much greater effects on wellbeing than shorter ones (Sin and Lyubomirsky, 2009). So, the trick is to keep your students repeating their favourite activities week after week and find different ways of performing them so that they don't get bored.

Another important factor that influences the effectiveness of an intervention is the variety of activities introduced (Lyubomirsky and Layous, 2013). This variety refers to using one activity in many different ways. For example, when doing acts of kindness it is more beneficial to do varied acts than repeat the same act of kindness each time we practise it (Sheldon et al., 2013), as well as doing various activities at the same time. Similarly, when participants were asked to make a positive life change (e.g., walking to school, instead of being dropped off), those whose activities varied during the time of an experiment received more gains from the activity (Sheldon et al., 2013). However, please note that being involved in too many exercises at the same time might not be beneficial. In an online wellbeing experiment, participants who practised four exercises received greater wellbeing gains and reductions in depression than those who did no activities or who did six activities in the same period of time (Schueller and Parks, 2012). This is why again, balance is required when practising wellbeing interventions.

The reason that variety is good for us is the issue of adaptation. Adaptation is part of our daily life. When we experience defeat or challenging life events, sooner or later most of us adapt to our changed circumstances (Lyubomirsky, 2011). The same applies to positive life events, including practising some wellbeing interventions. No matter how great things are today, next week or next month, we might start taking our good fortune for granted, or the gratitude activity we were practising will no longer have as much of a positive effect as it used to. The good news is that most of us are usually happy and well, so even if an activity doesn't work for us anymore or we start taking our life for granted, most of us return to a high enough level of wellness (Diener et al., 2006). However, to maintain higher levels of wellbeing, practising a variety of activities will keep us engaged with them more.

Another reason that a variety of interventions should be practiced is that it is the collection of activities that boosts our wellbeing the most (Schotanus-Dijkstra et al., 2017). In this experiment, the researchers examined the effect of various email-guided interventions on the experiences of positive emotions, the use of strengths, optimism, self-compassion, resilience and positive relations. They also explored how these processes mediate mental wellbeing, anxiety and depressive symptoms. When they looked at how individual interventions mediated wellbeing, they found small to moderate effects. When they considered the cumulative impact of the interventions practised, they found they had a considerable impact on enhancing wellbeing and reducing anxiety and depression. This study showed us the importance of introducing many components of wellbeing together, rather than sticking with just one.

As much as dosage, and variety matters, so does the support for the activities we do (Lyubomirsky and Layous, 2013). This is where a whole-school approach comes in offering students support not only in school by all teachers but also with parents who are aware of the activities their children are involved in and reinforce them at home. Peer support, however, is of upmost importance. When peer support was introduced while carrying out wellbeing interventions, participants showed greater improvements in their wellbeing

Teachers play an important role in strategy implementation as their involvement in teaching wellbeing is not only welcomed by students but also more effective than bringing in an expert from the outside (Waters et al., 2015). It may be because there is trust established between students and teachers that allows students to listen to their teacher and take on board what he or she says. It could be because teachers know their students well; therefore, the activities they select for them may be most appropriate to the class they work with. It may also be the case that the relationship between teachers and students changes when they start discussing wellbeing. Teachers may be more reflective about the impact of their words and actions on students and students listen to teachers talk about wellbeing and realise that they care. Regardless of the reason, teachers make wellbeing interventions more impactful for students, and this approach appears to have a positive effect on students' health (Skar et al., 2015). Therefore, actively engaging teachers in the school's wellbeing strategy will make the interventions more effective for students.

The person

The effect of an intervention is significantly higher when participants have a strong belief that the intervention will work for them and are motivated to engage with it (Lyubomirsky and Layous, 2013). For example, an online wellbeing study showed that a series of positive psychology interventions created significant changes in wellbeing and participants' experiences of depression (Seligman et al., 2005). However, when that study was replicated a few years later with a group of adults (Mongrain and Anselmo-Matthews, 2012) and adolescents (Khanna and Singh, 2019), their results were more modest, not showing a reduction in depression, as previously noted. What differentiated the first group from the rest was their interest in positive psychology and self-development. The group that had the highest increase in wellbeing and decrease in depression had a motivation to do the activities as they had signed up to a self-help happiness website. The other groups were randomly selected without any specific knowledge of positive psychology or interest in enhancing their wellbeing. This is why students who want to participate in a programme, intervention or any other activities associated with the wellbeing strategy will be more likely to increase their wellbeing in comparison to those who have had their wellbeing intervention assigned to them.

What can we do to encourage students to participate in a school's wellbeing strategy? We live in a world where other people's opinions matter. If a film on Netflix scores three stars out of five, we choose not to watch it, because we trust that others got it right, even though they are strangers to us. The same process applies when administering wellbeing programmes or interventions in our schools. When researchers showed a group testimonials about the effectiveness of a wellbeing intervention, it amplified their wellbeing, in comparison to a group that did not read any testimonials (Layous et al., 2013). This is not unusual and there are two processes that influenced these results. Firstly, it is down to groupthink, which is a mode of thinking that makes us choose conformity, even when faced with contradicting facts (Janis, 1973). In other words, while we might not trust individuals, we do trust the opinion of crowds, even if their thinking is unreasonable. Secondly, self-efficacy improves our chances of succeeding at tasks, as we have a stronger belief that we can do it (Bandura and Albert, 1978). One of the best ways to enhance our self-efficacy is by listening to what other people have done (vicarious efficacy) and how it helped them. Surely, if others could do it, so can we. This is possibly why the testimonials help students to engage more in the wellbeing activities and should be gathered throughout the process and perhaps shared with the community during school gatherings or on notice boards.

For activities to have a positive effect, a student completing them needs to make an effort, as more effort is associated with better results (Layous et al., 2013). What helps students make more effort is knowing that their effort will pay back (Lyubomirsky and Layous, 2013). That belief acts as a motivation to do it. At the same time, effort-making is not only due to our motivation. In order to decide whether or not we want to engage with a task, such as a wellbeing intervention, we weigh the effort we need to put into it against the value it offers us, and when mentally or physically exhausted, we tend to select the low-hanging fruit and an activity that does not require putting in a huge amount effort (Massar et al., 2018). In other words, effort-making is not only down to the individuals' motivation, but also their state of mind. This is why a selection of activities that require varied levels of effort need to be offered to students when designing a strategy for wellbeing, especially, during demanding times during the school-year, such as exams.

Encouraging students to make an effort always makes me a little uncomfortable, as it is placing a huge pressure on the school community to take responsibility for their own wellbeing. By pointing out the importance of effort what we are saying indirectly is that "*if you are unhappy it is your fault, because you did not make enough effort to change it.*" This is not a good message to pass on to young people, even though sometimes it may be true. Instead, what we may consider saying is that while their personal effort is important, there are other factors that matter too. It is the mixture of all the elements that makes a community's wellbeing thrive.

Take-aways for the school's wellbeing strategy

- It is important to understand the mechanisms behind implementing programmes and wellbeing interventions.
- Consider the individual differences of your school community, as well as the demands at various points of time during the school-year.
- Ensure that the community have a free choice of selecting a wellbeing intervention that works best for them, as well as the frequency of practice.
- Encourage the school community to engage in a variety of interventions and support each other.
- Ensure that you have a clear wellbeing framework for your school and that your strategy includes a multidisciplinary approach to wellbeing.

References

Ahmed, N. & Schwind, J. K. 2018. Supporting the wellbeing of inner-city middle-school students through mindful and creative reflective activities. *Reflective Practice*, 19, 412–425.

Bandura, A. & Albert, B. 1978. Self-efficacy: Toward a unifying theory of behavioral change. *Advances in Behaviour Research and Therapy*, 1, 139–161.

Barry, M. M., Clarke, A. M., Jenkins, R. & Patel, V. 2013. A systematic review of the effectiveness of mental health promotion interventions for young people in low and middle income countries. *BMC Public Health*, 13, 1–19.

Baumeister, R. F. & Vohs, K. D. 2007. Self-regulation, ego depletion, and motivation. *Social and Personality Psychology Compass*, 1, 115–128.

Belsky, J., Jonassaint, C., Pluess, M., Stanton, M., Brummett, B. & Williams, R. 2009. Vulnerability genes or plasticity genes? *Molecular Psychiatry*, 14, 746–754.

Boniwell, I. 2017. *Positive actions: Evidence-based positive psychology intervention cards*. Paris: Positron.

Boniwell, I. & Tunariu, A. D. 2019. *Positive psychology theory, research and applications*. London: Open University Press.

Boniwell, I. & Zimbardo, P. G. 2004. Balancing time perspective in pursuit of optimal functioning. In: Linley, P. A. & Joseph, S. (eds.), *Positive psychology in practice*. Hoboken, NJ: John Wiley & Sons, Inc.

Boniwell, I., Osin, E. & Sircova, A. 2014. Introducing time perspective coaching: A new approach to improve time management and enhance well-being. *International Journal of Evidence Based Coaching & Mentoring*, 12, 24–40.

Britton, W. B. 2019. Can mindfulness be too much of a good thing? The value of a middle way. *Current Opinion in Psychology*, 28, 159–165.

Brown, N. J. L., Sokal, A. D. & Friedman, H. L. 2013. The complex dynamics of wishful thinking: The critical positivity ratio. *American Psychologist*, 68, 801–813.

Dejonckheere, E. & Bastian, B. 2020. Perceiving social pressure not to feel negative is linked to a more negative self-concept. *Journal of Happiness Studies: An Interdisciplinary Forum on Subjective Well-Being*. doi:10.1007/s10902-020-00246-4.

Diener, E., Suh, E. M., Lucas, R. E. & Smith, H. L. 1999. Subjective well-being: Three decades of progress. *Psychological Bulletin*, 125, 276–302.

Diener, E., Lucas, R. E. & Scollon, C. N. 2006. Beyond the hedonic treadmill: Revising the adaptation theory of well-being. *American Psychologist*, 61, 305–314.

Ford, B. Q., Shallcross, A. J., Mauss, I. B., Floerke, V. A. & Gruber, J. 2014. Desperately seeking happiness: Valuing happiness is associated with symptoms and diagnosis of depression. *Journal of Social & Clinical Psychology*, 33, 890–905.

Ford, B. Q., Dmitrieva, J. O., Heller, D., Chentsova-Dutton, Y., Grossmann, I., Tamir, M., Yukiko, U., Koopmann-Holm, B., Floerke, V. A., Uhrig, M., Bokhan, T. & Mauss, I. B. 2015. Culture shapes whether the pursuit of happiness predicts higher or lower well-being. *Journal of Experimental Psychology: General*, 144, 1053–1062.

Fordyce, M. W. 1977. Development of a program to increase personal happiness. *Journal of Counseling Psychology*, 24, 511–521.

Fordyce, M. W. 1983. A program to increase happiness: Further studies. *Journal of Counseling Psychology*, 30, 483–498.

Fredrickson, B. L. & Losada, M. F. 2005. Positive affect and the complex dynamics of human flourishing. *American Psychologist*, 60, 678–686.

Fredrickson, B. L. & Losada, M. F. 2013. 'Positive affect and the complex dynamics of human flourishing': Correction to Fredrickson and Losada (2005). *American Psychologist*, 68, 822–822.

Gentzler, A. L., Palmer, C. A., Ford, B. Q., Moran, K. M. & Mauss, I. B. 2019. Valuing happiness in youth: Associations with depressive symptoms and well-being. *Journal of Applied Developmental Psychology*, 62, 220–230.

Greven, C. U., Lionetti, F., Booth, C., Aron, E. N., Fox, E., Schendan, H. E., Pluess, M., Bruining, H., Acevedo, B., Bijttebier, P. & Homberg, J. 2019. Sensory processing sensitivity in the context of environmental sensitivity: A critical review and development of research agenda. *Neuroscience and Biobehavioral Reviews*, 98, 287–305.

Hung, T. T. M., Chiang, V. C. L., Dawson, A. & Lee, R. L. T. 2014. Understanding of factors that enable health promoters in implementing health-promoting schools: A systematic review and narrative synthesis of qualitative evidence. *PLoS ONE*, 9, 1–13.

Janis, I.L. 1973. *Victims of groupthink* (2nd Ed). Boston: Houghton Mifflin.

Kennedy, E. 2013. Orchids and dandelions: How some children are more susceptible to environmental influences for better or worse and the implications for child development. *Clinical Child Psychology and Psychiatry*, 18, 319–321.

Khanna, P. & Singh, K. 2019. Do all positive psychology exercises work for everyone? Replication of seligman et al's (2005) interventions among adolescents. *Psychological Studies*, 64, 1–19.

Ko, K., Margolis, S., Revord, J. & Lyubomirsky, S. 2019. Comparing the effects of performing and recalling acts of kindness. *The Journal of Positive Psychology*. doi:10.1080/17439760.2019.1663252.

Layous, K., Lee, H., Choi, I. & Lyubomirsky, S. 2013. Culture matters when designing a successful happiness-increasing activity: A comparison of the United States and South Korea. *Journal of Cross-Cultural Psychology*, 44, 1294–1303.

Lichter, S., Haye, K. & Kammann, R. 1980. Increasing happiness through cognitive retraining. *New Zealand Psychologist*, 9, 57–64.

Lionetti, F., Aron, A., Aron, E. N., Burns, G. L., Jagiellowicz, J. & Pluess, M. 2018. Dandelions, tulips and orchids: Evidence for the existence of low-sensitive, medium-sensitive and high-sensitive individuals. *Translational Psychiatry*, 8, 24.

Luong, G., Wrzus, C., Wagner, G. G. & Riediger, M. 2016. When bad moods may not be so bad: Valuing negative affect is associated with weakened affect–health links. *Emotion*, 16, 387–401.

Lyubomirsky, S. 2007. *The how of happiness: A scientific approach to getting the life you want*. New York, NY: Penguin Press.

Lyubomirsky, S. 2011. Hedonic adaptation to positive and negative experiences. In: Folkman, S. (ed.), *The Oxford handbook of stress, health, and coping*. New York, NY: Oxford University Press.

Lyubomirsky, S. & Layous, K. 2013. How do simple positive activities increase well-being? *Current Directions in Psychological Science*, 22, 57–62.

Lyubomirsky, S., Sheldon, K. M. & Schkade, D. 2005. Pursuing happiness: The architecture of sustainable change. *Review of General Psychology*, 9, 111–131.

Lyubomirsky, S., Sousa, L. & Dickerhoof, R. 2006. The costs and benefits of writing, talking, and thinking about life's triumphs and defeats. *Journal of Personality and Social Psychology*, 90, 692–708.

Massar, S. A. A., Csathó, Á. & Van der Linden, D. 2018. Quantifying the motivational effects of cognitive fatigue through effort-based decision making. *Frontiers in Psychology*, 9, Article 843.

Mauss, I. B., Tamir, M., Anderson, C. L. & Savino, N. S. 2011. Can seeking happiness make people unhappy? Paradoxical effects of valuing happiness. *Emotion*, 11, 807–815.

Mauss, I. B., Savino, N. S., Anderson, C. L., Weisbuch, M., Tamir, M. & Laudenslager, M. L. 2012. The pursuit of happiness can be lonely. *Emotion*, 12, 908–912.

Mcguirk, L., Kuppens, P., Kingston, R. & Bastian, B. 2018. Does a culture of happiness increase rumination over failure? *Emotion*, 18, 755–764.

Mongrain, M. & Anselmo-Matthews, T. 2012. Do positive psychology exercises work? A replication of Seligman et al. (2005). *Journal of Clinical Psychology*, 68, 382–389.

Mortari, L. & Ubbiali, M. 2017. The "MelArete" project: Educating children to the ethics of virtue and of care. *European Journal of Educational Research*, 6, 269–278.

Myers, D. G. 2000. The funds, friends, and faith of happy people. *American Psychologist*, 55, 56–67.

Nelson, S. K., Layous, K., Cole, S. W. & Lyubomirsky, S. 2016. Do unto others or treat yourself? The effects of prosocial and self-focused behavior on psychological flourishing. *Emotion*, 16, 850–861.

Nocentini, A., Menesini, E. & Pluess, M. 2018. The personality trait of environmental sensitivity predicts children's positive response to school-based antibullying intervention. *Clinical Psychological Science*, 6, 848–859.

Norem, J. K. 2001. *The positive power of negative thinking: Using defensive pessimism to manage anxiety and perform at your peak*. New York, NY: Basic Books.

O'Toole, C. 2017. Towards dynamic and interdisciplinary frameworks for school-based mental health promotion. *Health Education*, 117, 452–468.

Parks, A. C., Della Porta, M. D., Pierce, R. S., Zilca, R. & Lyubomirsky, S. 2012. Pursuing happiness in everyday life: The characteristics and behaviors of online happiness seekers. *Emotion*, 12, 1222–1234.

Pluess, M. & Boniwell, I. 2015. Sensory-processing sensitivity predicts treatment response to a school-based depression prevention program: Evidence of vantage sensitivity. *Personality and Individual Differences*, 82, 40–45.

Pluess, M., Assary, E., Lionetti, F., Lester, K. J., Krapohl, E., Aron, E. N. & Aron, A. 2018. Environmental sensitivity in children: Development of the highly sensitive child scale and identification of sensitivity groups. *Developmental Psychology*, 54, 51–70.

Roffey, S. 2015. Becoming an agent of change for school and student well-being. *Educational & Child Psychology*, 32, 21–30.

Rütten, A., Frahsa, A. A. F. F. D., Abel, T., Bergmann, M., Leeuw, E. D., Hunter, D., Jansen, M., King, A. & Potvin, L. 2019. Co-producing active lifestyles as whole-system-approach: Theory, intervention and knowledge-to-action implications. *Health Promotion International*, 34, 47–59.

Ryan, R. M. & Deci, E. L. 2000. Self-determination theory and the facilitation of intrinsic motivation, social development, and well-being. *American Psychologist*, 55, 68–78.

Schooler, J., Ariely, D. & Loewenstein, G. 2003. The explicit pursuit and assessment of happiness can be self-defeating. In: Brocas, I. & Carrillo, J. D. (eds.), *The psychology of economic decisions*. Oxford: Oxford University Press.

Schotanus-Dijkstra, M., Drossaert, C. H. C., Pieterse, M. E., Boon, B., Walburg, J. A. & Bohlmeijerb, E. T. 2017. An early intervention to promote well-being and flourishing and reduce anxiety and depression: A randomized controlled trial. *Internet Interventions*, 9, 15–24.

Schueller, S. M. 2010. Preferences for positive psychology exercises. *The Journal of Positive Psychology*, 5, 192–203.

Schueller, S. M. & Parks, A. C. 2012. Disseminating self-help: Positive psychology exercises in an online trial. *Journal of Medical Internet Research*, 14, 8–18.

Schueller, S. M. & Parks, A. C. 2014. The science of self-help: Translating positive psychology research into increased individual happiness. *European Psychologist*, 19, 145–155.

Schwartz, B. 2004. *The paradox of choice: Why more is less*. New York, NY: HarperCollins.

Schwartz, B., Ward, A. & Lyubomirsky, S. 2002. Maximizing versus satisficing: Happiness is a matter of choice. *Journal of Personality and Social Psychology*, 83, 1178–1197.

Segerstrom, S. C. 2009. *The glass half-full: How optimists get what they want from life and pessimists can too*. London: Constable and Robinson.

Seligman, M. E. P. 2002. *Authentic happiness: Using the new positive psychology to realize your potential for lasting fulfillment*. New York, NY: Free Press.

Seligman, M. E. P. 2011. *Flourish: A visionary new understanding of happiness and well-being*. New York, NY: Atria.

Seligman, M. E. P., Steen, T. A., Park, N. & Peterson, C. 2005. Positive psychology progress: Empirical validation of interventions. *American Psychologist*, 60, 410–421.

Sheldon, K. M., Boehm, J. & Lyubomirsky, S. 2013. Variety is the spice of happiness: The hedonic adaptation prevention model. In: David, S. A., Boniwell, I. & Conley Ayers, A. (eds.), *The Oxford handbook of happiness*. New York, NY: Oxford University Press.

Shepherd, J., Garcia, J., Oliver, S., Harden, A., Rees, R., Brunton, G. & Oakley, A. 2002. *Barriers to, and facilitators of the health of young people: A systematic review of evidence on young people's views and on interventions in mental health, physical activity and healthy eating*. Vol. 2: Complete Report. London: EPPI-Centre, Social Science Research Unit, Institute of Education, University of London.

Silberman, J. 2007. Positive intervention self-selection: Developing models of what works for whom. *International Coaching Psychology Review*, 2, 70–77.

Sin, N. L. & Lyubomirsky, S. 2009. Enhancing well-being and alleviating depressive symptoms with positive psychology interventions: A practice-friendly meta-analysis. *Part of special issue on: Positive Psychology in Clinical Practice*, 65, 467–487.

Skar, M., Kirstein, E. & Kapur, A. 2015. Lessons learnt from school-based health promotion projects in low- and middle-income countries. *Child: Care, Health & Development*, 41, 1114–1123.

Svane, D., Evans, N. & Carter, M.-A. 2019. Wicked wellbeing: Examining the disconnect between the rhetoric and reality of wellbeing interventions in schools. *Australian Journal of Education*, 63, 209–231.

Trinder, H. & Salkovskis, P. M. 1994. Personally relevant intrusions outside the laboratory: Long-term suppression increases intrusion. *Behaviour Research and Therapy*, 32, 833–842.

Tseng, W.-C. 2017. An intervention using LEGO® SERIOUS PLAY® on fostering narrative identity among economically disadvantaged college students in Taiwan. *Journal of College Student Development*, 58, 264–282.

Waters, L., Barsky, A., Ridd, A. & Allen, K. 2015. Contemplative education: A systematic, evidence-based review of the effect of meditation interventions in schools. *Educational Psychology Review*, 27, 103–134.

Wegner, D. M. 2011. When you put things out of mind, where do they go? In: Gernsbacher, M. A., Pew, R. W., Hough, L. M. & Pomerantz, J. R. (eds.), *Psychology and the real world: Essays illustrating fundamental contributions to society*. New York, NY: Worth Publishers.

Wehmeyer, M. L., Shogren, K. A., Little, T. D. & Lopez, S. J. 2017. *Development of self-determination through the life-course*. New York, NY: Springer Science + Business Media.

Wellenzohn, S., Proyer, R. T. & Ruch, W. 2016. Humor-based online positive psychology interventions: A randomized placebo-controlled long-term trial. *The Journal of Positive Psychology*, 11, 584–594.

Willoughby, G. & Tosey, P. 2007. Imagine 'meadfield': Appreciative inquiry as a process for leading school improvement. *Educational Management Administration & Leadership*, 35, 499–520.

Zimbardo, P. & Boyd, J. 2008. *The time paradox: The new psychology of time that will change your life*. New York, NY: Free Press.

Zimbardo, P., Sword, R. & Sword, R. 2012. *The time cure: Overcoming PTSD with the new psychology of time perspective therapy*. San Francisco, CA: Jossey-Bass.

CHAPTER 5

A review of established school wellbeing programmes

Twenty years ago, before the explosion of wellbeing in school began, when researchers tried to create a list of wellbeing programmes available for young people in both school and other settings, they found over 800 of them (Harden et al., 2001). Nowadays, there are thousands of various programmes available in countries worldwide. Many of the evaluated, evidence-based programmes come from the field of Positive Education. Some are showcased during an annual Positive Education Festival organised by the International Positive Education Network (IPEN). The objective of this chapter is not to list them, but to help you discern the usefulness of any programmes that come your way. In order to demonstrate how to do it, we will review a few of the wellbeing programmes applied in primary and secondary education.

Here is a list of criteria I would use when evaluating each programme:

1. The audience
2. Wellbeing elements
3. Cultural fit
4. Effectiveness

Let me go through these one-by-one.

The audience

Many of the programmes are designed based on children's age and their level of development. Therefore, there are specific programmes for children in pre-school, primary and secondary schools. In addition to this, there are also programmes available for specific school communities, such as boy-only schools. Programmes designed for boys and young men are different in that they use a language better understood by males, topics that incorporate masculine-specific theories and interventions, which help boys develop a healthy masculine identity (Gwyther et al., 2019). For example the *Rock and Water Programme* is an Australian programme designed for boys; the main aim of which is to help them manage their negative emotions, specifically anger and aggression and through this improve boys' engagement in school (Edwards et al., 2017). To date, the programme has been applied with over two million school children. This is just one example of selecting an audience-specific wellbeing programmes.

There are also wellbeing programmes designed for school minorities, such as children of soldiers (Brendel et al., 2014), young people whose parents were diagnosed with a serious illness (Skeen et al., 2017), or for parents of children with disability (Moody et al., 2019). These programme assist young people and their parents in coping with a specific adversity or circumstances they experience. This is why, when selecting a programme, it is important to ensure its suitability for your school community or specific subgroups of the community. However, care needs to be taken to ensure that the students do not feel excluded or victimised for their disability or other circumstances that put them in a minority group.

Wellbeing elements

When you review the content of potential programmes, you might want to note what aspects of wellbeing it addresses and how it matches your schools' wellbeing strategy. There is not much point in introducing a programme just because its ticks off the *wellbeing box* on your school agenda. If it is not aligned with your school's wellbeing strategy, a more suitable programme should be selected.

Some programmes address aspects of resilience, such as the *Penn Resiliency* Program, me which was designed to prevent depression, anxiety and externalising behaviours in young people (Reivich and Gillham, 2010). The programme was created in the early 1990s and applies positive psychology research on optimism, as young people are guided through a process of overcoming their pessimistic thoughts and apply cognitive-behavioural and social problem-solving techniques. The *Bounce Back!* programme (McGrath, 2000) uses the same optimism theory in its activities with primary school children and some cognitive and emotional methods on coping with. Another element they specifically address is bullying. The *SPARK* programme is yet another attempt to enhance students' resilience skills, including the concept of post-traumatic growth (Pluess et al., 2017), whereas the *ENTRÉE* programme is a European teacher resilience project delivering modules, such as stress management, relationships, resilience and the education for wellbeing (Fernandes et al., 2019). Other programmes such as the *Friends for Life* uses cognitive behavioural techniques to cope with the symptoms of anxiety. *MoodGym* is an online programme for young people helping them cope with depression (Twomey and O'Reilly, 2017), whereas the *Mindfulness-based Stress Reduction* Programme (Kabat-Zinn, 2005) is focused on reducing stress; however, many of the outcomes are reported to reduce depression, anxiety and physical illness (Grossman et al., 2004). When applied with teachers, mindfulness has improved the educators' symptoms of insomnia (Frank et al., 2015).

Each one of the programmes offers something unique and addresses different components of wellbeing. When selecting a programme for your school, you will consider programmes that are available in your geographic area; therefore, you will be somewhat limited as to the choices you make. However, enquire into the content and what aspect of wellbeing the programme addresses, as this will help you make a decision as to whether your school needs it or not.

Cultural fit

There are some countries that are significantly more active in designing evidence-based wellbeing programmes for schools, such as the USA or Australia. Researchers and practitioners often wonder whether programmes created in one cultural context can be easily transferable to another cultural context. A review of programmes found that in general it is possible, as for example, the US-based programmes have shown similar effects in European contexts and Australian contexts (Weare and Nind, 2011). However, when specific programmes are considered, not all of them are effective.

An example comes from the *Penn Resiliency Programme* which was initially developed in the US, and further tested in the UK, where it showed positive results (Challen et al., 2014). Yet, while its Dutch version "Ob Volle Kracht" showed encouraging short-term effects (Wijnhoven et al., 2014), it was less effective long-term (Tak et al., 2016). This is why it is crucial that when selecting a programme, schools consider the countries where it was previously tested. If an evaluation has not been carried out in your country, you may request that it is done in your specific school, as a pilot, to allow for the assessment of the effectiveness of the programme.

Another important thing to consider is the adaptation of the programme to the specific culture where it is delivered. The culture may include the country where it is delivered or specific population of the country. For example, in Australia, one of the most prominent wellbeing programmes for school children in the 2000s was *MindMatters* (Services, 2000). Even though it tackled the issue of diversity and wellbeing in relation to Aboriginal and Torres Strait Islanders, it needed to be further adapted in some Indigenous communities (Osborne, 2013). Similarly, in the US, the *New Beginning Parent Programme* supporting their wellbeing post-divorce was devised, and the researchers identified cultural intricacies relating to a specific Asian-American population, such as mothers' challenges in negotiating former in-laws involvement, which was not as salient in non-Asian-American population (Zhou et al., 2014). This is why it is crucial that when implementing a wellbeing programme, the cultural differences are considered by schools.

Effectiveness

In order to identify how effective a programme is, we need to consider what type of assessment the creators of the programme used to evaluate it. Was the assessment based merely on students' enjoyment of the programme content? If so it is good to know, but there are other type of evaluations that may be considered. For example, some programmes evaluate changes in students' behaviour observed by their teachers or parents. Other programmes provide information about changes in students' self-reported attitudes, thoughts, emotions and behaviours. The more comprehensive and versatile the assessments, the more we know about the effect of the programme on students.

Another important point to consider is the quality and quantity of research that was carried out for each programme. Some programmes claim to be evidence-based after conducting a single study with a small number of participants. Other programmes were evaluated in many studies with large groups of children across various geographical locations. When a programme boasts extensive research, their results are often compared in a meta-analysis to identify the effect of the multiple programme-delivery on various aspects of wellbeing and other outcomes, or to contrast the effects of one programme with another. Programmes that have reached this level offer most evidence about their effectiveness and help us understand in what way they may be useful to our school community.

Let's take *Friends for Life* (Barrett et al., 1999) as an example, endorsed by the World Health Organisation in 2004 (WHO, 2004), as the only school-based anxiety prevention programme recommended at that time. Yet, a decade later when a meta-analysis of the programme was carried out, it identified that the research behind it was not rigorous enough (Maggin and Johnson, 2014). Furthermore, all the studies that were designed poorly were rejected, and from 50 studies, only 17 were selected showing that pupils with low-risk for developing anxiety reported no statistically significant reduction in their anxiety after completing the programme, making the efficacy of *Friends for Life* questionable. Following on from this, the programme director, Paula Barrett, wrote a response to the researchers criticising the methodology used in the meta-analysis (Barrett et al., 2017). Further research needs to be carried out to identify the overall effect of this programme.

In comparison, the *Zippy Friends* (Children, 2020, Partnership for Life, 2020) is a programme designed mainly for pre-school, which helps children cope more effectively with daily life challenges programme. There are some individual studies showing promising results about it reducing bullying and improving academic skills (Holen et al., 2013), helping children cope and reducing externalising behaviours (Mishara and Ystgaard, 2006), helpful for children during a transition from the kindergarten to primary school (Monkevicienė et al., 2006); however, there is not enough research published about it in the form of a meta-analysis. More studies need to be published to identify the effect of the programme.

Another example comes from the *Penn Resilience Program* (Reivich and Gillham, 2010), which was designed to prevent depression and help young people reduce their symptoms of depression. In a meta-analytic study, the results showed that not only was it effective in doing so, but the effectiveness was sustained for at least 12 months and in some cases longer (Brunwasser et al., 2009). The good news is that in a recent meta-analysis including the comparison of various resilience-oriented programmes around the world, the researchers found that programmes based on the *Penn Resiliency Programme* content had the highest levels of decreased depression (Ma et al., 2020).

These three examples of programmes show the importance of asking the programme providers for research data. Just because the programme has the content we want and find useful does not mean it will be effective for our students. When you are choosing a programme for your school, I recommend you ask for the specific evidence behind the programme you consider, a copy of the research paper as well as asking what the limitations of the studies are or what criticism are there about the programme evaluation. It may provide you with some interesting findings that help you make an informed decision.

Take-aways for the school's wellbeing strategy

- Make sure that if you choose to select an existing wellbeing programme that it is aligned with your school's wellbeing framework and strategy.
- Make sure that the programme has been evaluated well and provides evidence that it indeed enhances students' wellbeing and does not harm them.
- Follow the steps towards the comprehensive programme evaluation.

References

Barrett, P. M., Lowry-Webster, H. M. & Turner, C. M. 1999. *FRIENDS Program Social Validity and Treatment Integrity Scales*. Brisbane: Australia, Australian Academic Press.

Barrett, P. M., Cooper, M., Stallard, P., Zeggio, L. & Gallegos-Guajardo, J. 2017. Effective evaluation of the FRIENDS Anxiety Prevention Program in school settings: A response to Maggin and Johnson. *Education & Treatment of Children*, 40, 99–110.

Brendel, K. E., Maynard, B. R., Albright, D. L. & Bellomo, M. 2014. Effects of school-based interventions with US military-connected children: A systematic review. *Research on Social Work Practice*, 24, 649–658.

Brunwasser, S. M., Gilham, J. E. & Kim, E. S. 2009. A meta-analytic review of the Penn Resiliency Program's effect on depressive symptoms. *Journal of Consulting & Clinical Psychology*, 77, 1042–1054.

Challen, A. R., Machin, S. J. & Gillham, J. E. 2014. The UK Resilience Programme: A school-based universal nonrandomized pragmatic controlled trial. *Journal of Consulting and Clinical Psychology*, 82, 75–89.

Children, P. F. 2020. *Our skills for life programmes for schools* [Online]. Available: https://www.partnershipforchildren.org.uk/ [Accessed 23rd Sep 2020].

Edwards, P., Mortel, T. & Stevens, J. 2017. Addressing engagement, anger and aggression through the Rock Water Program: Rural adolescent males' perceptions. *Australian Journal of Rural Health*, 25, 241–245.

Fernandes, L., Peixoto, F., Gouveia, M. J., Silva, J. C. & Wosnitza, M. 2019. Fostering teachers' resilience and well-being through professional learning: Effects from a training programme. *Australian Educational Researcher*, 46, 681–698.

Frank, J. L., Reibel, D., Broderick, P., Cantrell, T. & Metz, S. 2015. The effectiveness of mindfulness-based stress reduction on educator stress and well-being: Results from a pilot study. *Mindfulness*, 6, 208–216.

Grossman, P., Niemann, L., Schmidt, S. & Walach, H. 2004. Mindfulness-based stress reduction and health benefits: A meta-analysis. *Journal of Psychosomatic Research*, 57, 35–43.

Gwyther, K., Swann, R., Casey, K., Purcell, R. & Rice, S. M. 2019. Developing young men's wellbeing through community and school-based programs: A systematic review. *PLoS ONE*, 14, 1–20.

Harden, A., Rees, R., Shepherd, J., Brunton, G., Oliver, S. & Oakley, A. 2001. *Young People and Mental Health: A Systematic Review of Barriers and Facilitators*. London: EPPI-Centre, Social Science Research Unit.

Holen, S., Waaktaar, T., Lervåg, A. & Ystgaard, M. 2013. Implementing a Universal Stress Management Program for young school children: Are there classroom climate or academic effects? *Scandinavian Journal of Educational Research*, 57, 420–444.

Kabat-Zinn, J. 2005. *Full Catastrophe Living: Using the Wisdom of Your Body and Mind to Face Stress, Pain, and Illness*, 15th anniversary ed. New York: Delta Trade Paperback/Bantam Dell.

Ma, L., Zhang, Y., Huang, C. & Cui, Z. 2020. Resilience-oriented cognitive behavioral interventions for depressive symptoms in children and adolescents: A meta-analytic review. *Journal of Affective Disorders*, 270, 150–164.

Maggin, D. M. & Johnson, A. H. 2014. A meta-analytic evaluation of the FRIENDS Program for preventing anxiety in student populations. *Education & Treatment of Children*, 37, 277–306.

McGrath, H. 2000. *The BOUNCE BACK! Resiliency Program: A Pilot Study*, American Educational Research Association, New Orleans.

Mishara, B. L. & Ystgaard, M. 2006. Effectiveness of a Mental Health Promotion Program to improve coping skills in young children: "Zippy's Friends". *Early Childhood Research Quarterly*, 21, 110–123.

Monkevicien, O., Mishara, B. & Dufour, S. 2006. Effects of the Zippy's Friends Programme on children's coping abilities during the transition from kindergarten to elementary school. *Early Childhood Education Journal*, 34, 53–60.

Moody, E. J., Kaiser, K., Sharp, D., Kubicek, L. F., Rigles, B., Davis, J., McSwegin, S., D'Abreu, L. C. & Rosenberg, C. R. 2019. Improving family functioning following diagnosis of ASD: A randomized trial of a Parent Mentorship Program. *Journal of Child & Family Studies*, 28, 424–435.

Osborne, S. 2013. Kulintja Nganampa Maa-kunpuntjaku (strengthening our thinking): Place-based approaches to mental health and wellbeing in Anangu schools. *Australian Journal of Indigenous Education*, 42, 182–193.

Partnership for Life. 2020. Our skills for life programmes for schools [Online]. Available: https://www.partnershipforchildren.org.uk/ [Accessed].

Pluess, M., Boniwell, I., Hefferon, K. & Tunariu, A. 2017. Preliminary evaluation of a school-based resilience-promoting intervention in a high-risk population: Application of an exploratory two-cohort treatment/control design. *PLoS ONE*, 12, 1–18.

Reivich, K. & Gillham, J. 2010. Building resilience in youth: The Penn Resiliency Program. *Communique*, 38, 1–17.

Services., T. M. H. B. O. T. A. C. D. O. A. F. 2000. SchoolMatters: mapping and managing mental health in schools. *The MindMatters resource kit*. Canberra, Australia: Commonwealth Department of Health and Aged Care.

Skeen, S. A., Sherr, L., Croome, N., Gandhi, N., Roberts, K. J., Macedo, A. & Tomlinson, M. 2017. Interventions to improve psychosocial well-being for children affected by HIV and AIDS: A systematic review. *Vulnerable Children & Youth Studies*, 12, 91–116.

Tak, Y. R., Lichtwarck-Aschoff, A., Gillham, J. E., Zundert, R. M. P. & Engels, R. C. M. E. 2016. Universal school-based depression prevention 'Op Volle Kracht': A longitudinal cluster randomized controlled trial. *Journal of Abnormal Child Psychology*, 44, 949–961.

Twomey, C. & O'Reilly, G. 2017. Effectiveness of a freely available computerised cognitive behavioural therapy programme (MoodGYM) for depression: Meta-analysis. *Australian and New Zealand Journal of Psychiatry*, 51, 260–269.

Weare, K. & Nind, M. 2011. Mental health promotion and problem prevention in schools: What does the evidence say? *Health Promotion International*, 26, 29–69.

WHO. 2004. *Prevention of Mental Disorders: Effective Interventions and Policy Options*. Geneva: WHO.

Wijnhoven, L., Creemers, D., Vermulst, A., Scholte, R. & Engels, R. 2014. Randomized controlled trial testing the effectiveness of a Depression Prevention Program ('Op Volle Kracht') among adolescent girls with elevated depressive symptoms. *Journal of Abnormal Child Psychology*, 42, 217–228.

Zhou, Q., Chen, S. H., Cookston, J. T. & Wolchik, S. 2014. Evaluating the cultural fit of the New Beginnings Parent Program for divorced Asian American mothers: A pilot study. *Asian American Journal of Psychology*, 5, 126–133.

CHAPTER 6

Your guide to making the best-informed decisions

I recently worked with a school leader who looks after a large secondary school community. She was trying to figure out the best way to create a wellbeing strategy in her school. Over the years, she has delivered a lot of ad hoc programmes and interventions, but was doubtful as to their effectiveness. We decided to go through this process differently and not only start by identifying students' needs, but also do it using a strength-based model, which was inspired by the Appreciative Inquiry model (Cooperrider and McQuaid, 2012) as well as research on what successful teams do differently when implementing health interventions in school communities (Leiva et al., 2020).

The school CARES model for creating a comprehensive wellbeing strategy is an alternative to a problem-solving model. It is not only easy to introduce, but also leaves everyone feeling inspired and motivated to make a positive change happen. CARES is a step-by-step acronym, in which C stands for Committee; A stands for Appreciation; R stands for Reverie; E stands for Explore and S stands for Share. Each one of these steps is discussed in Table 6.1.

Step 1: Committee

In some schools I have visited, there was only one person responsible for children's wellbeing. It was usually a teacher or a school leader who is interested in wellbeing. On a few occasions the school administrator took the role of coordinating wellbeing activities, not because they were specialists in the area, but because something needed to be done, and nobody else wanted to take on this task. In the school CARES model, however, it is a committee of dedicated stakeholders that aim to make a positive difference to their school community. That committee is composed of representatives of different groups, such as students, teachers, leaders, parents and other community members. The team selects a coordinator or a team leader who is responsible for progressing the creation and the execution of the strategy.

Usually, the successful teams comprise of individuals who have interest in wellbeing and a strong belief that they are able to do make a positive difference to the school

TABLE 6.1 The details of the school CARES model for implementing a wellbeing strategy

Stage	Objective	Outcome
1. Committee	Establishing a highly performing multidisciplinary team	− A team is selected − Trust and psychological safety is present − Democratic decision-making − Asking questions rather than advocating own ideas − Learning and applying individual strengths − Each member building community social network
2. Appreciate	Appreciating the strengths and needs of the school community	− Appreciate the strength of the school community − Appreciate the community social network and their individual strengths − Appreciate what is needed for the community the most to boost their wellbeing − Appreciate past research carried out with the community (evaluations and needs-analysis)
3. Reverie	Dreaming	− Dreaming of the best-case scenario
4. Explore	Brainstorming a multitude of ideas for the practical wellbeing school interventions	− Selecting a wellbeing framework − Brainstorming ideas for implementing the wellbeing framework in school across all levels of the community
5. Share	Sharing the vision and integrating it in the school community	− Sharing the vision − Sharing the dream − Sharing the initiatives − Sharing views of the community with the committee (feedback loop) − Sharing successes − Sharing evaluation

community (Leiva et al., 2020). They also have the knowledge of what wellbeing is all about or at least are willing to gain their knowledge via various resources, reading wellbeing-related books, such as this one, which will help them comprehend the bigger picture and more details perspectives on the science of wellbeing applied in education.

In order for a team to perform to the highest level of their potential, there needs to be trust and psychological safety between the committee members. Psychological safety is a belief that no matter what mistakes we make in the process of strategising for wellbeing, we will not be punished, embarrassed or made feel inadequate (Edmondson, 1999). When psychological safety is missing from a team, they are more likely to engage in self-protective behaviour, such as become defensive or mistrusting. On the other hand, when teachers experience psychological safety, they feel comfortable to raise their concerns, replace blame with curiosity and be more likely to voice their opinion in school (Bas and Tabancali, 2020). This is a fundamental need for a wellbeing committee to display, become the example for the rest of the school to follow and allow all the voices to be heard, so that the committee is fully a representative of the entire community and a safe environment, in which to make mistakes.

Some of the most successful teams leave their ego, their positions and their advocacy outside the door and come into a team's space with an open mind and many questions. Successful teams are more likely to actively exchange ideas and ask each other open and clarifying questions, rather than tell the group what needs to be done (Fredrickson and Losada, 2005). This is particularly pertinent in a committee situation, where all members should contribute to the final outcome, not only those in charge, or who speak the loudest. Each committee member represents their network, be it teachers, students, parents, board of directors or others. Their role is to give their network a voice. If members feel their ideas are not listened to, they will not be able to represent their network fully and soon their motivation and output will decline.

Some of the more successful committees that looked after the implementation of a wellbeing strategy practiced a democratic leadership style (Leiva et al., 2020). This means that while they had their roles to fill, such as the committee coordinators, they allowed everyone to participate in decision-making. They were also not swayed by the authority, that is, the school politics or government introducing changes. Unless the changes had to be implemented immediately, the committee considered them in due course.

In summary, a successful wellbeing strategy cannot be created unless a committee is established and maintained in a way that allows them to reach their potential. Each member needs to feel comfortable enough to share ideas without being ridiculed. Each member needs to use their strengths to shine and do the best they can to achieve the community's goal. And each member needs to be part of the decision-making process. This wellbeing-oriented attitude will become a solid basis for creating a wellbeing strategy.

Step 2: Appreciation

The second step in designing a wellbeing strategy is appreciating a community's strengths and needs. It is a process of identifying what the school has already done that worked well, and which can be replicated. It is a process that allows the committee to review the strengths of the school community, its members, its ideas and its capabilities. This process of appreciation will create the committee's self-efficacy, a belief that they can do this, which is an important element of making positive changes (Bandura and Albert, 1978). Without a belief that we can turn things around or introduce something new, we are not able to perform at the highest level of our potential.

Here are some of the questions that can be asked of the committee at this stage of the process:

- Can you share a story of when things were going great at school? What was happening? Who was there? How did it happen? What factors made it such a great experience?
- Think of the first time you came into the school, what did you like about it? What was your initial impression?
- Describe a time when the school community did something meaningful. What was it? Who was involved? What was the outcome? What would need to happen for us to do it again?

- What past interventions have been introduced and worked well in the school?
- What do you value the most about your school? Why? Who is involved? What do they do?
- Was there anyone in the past who did something extraordinary that enhanced everyone's wellbeing? What was it? What made it so extraordinary? How can we replicate it?

All these questions will help a committee create a landscape of positive events and network capabilities that already exist in the school's community and which need to be developed further. For example, say that one of the committee members, a student, reflects on a day when a teacher asked the class to talk about their hobbies. It created a great buzz in the classroom and brought the whole group a little closer. After hearing this story, the wellbeing committee decides to create a "hobby club" after school, where students can share their hobbies with others. This is what the process of story-sharing and subsequent decision-making looks like.

The appreciation of school's strengths is an important part of the strategy. Without the proper diagnostics as to the school's capacity to make a change, or the direction the change should take, the strategy will not be well integrated in the school (Leiva et al., 2020), nor will it be reflective of the school's values and cultures. This in-depth analysis of what the community appreciates provides us with the necessary foundations upon which the school's wellbeing strategy can be built.

Step 3: Reverie

The next step of the process is dreaming of the audacious outcomes for the process. This step should be carried out immediately after the step 2. When our mind is filled with positive stories about what the school community is doing well, it will allow us to dream an audacious dream of where we would like the school community to be three years time. Adapted from the the *Best Possible Self* intervention (King, 2001), each committee member shares their own vision of the best-case scenario for the school. If all went well and the school committee managed to accomplish all they are hoping to accomplish, what would the school's wellbeing initiatives or outcomes look like? This step of the process is essential for moving a school wellbeing strategy forward.

Step 4: Explore

This stage refers to exploring practical aspects of the wellbeing strategy implementation, which requires creativity. Creativity involves generating a combination of novel and useful ideas (Shalley et al., 2010). There are at least two types of creativity: (1) Creativity with a big-C, such as that of Picasso's, James Joyce's or Beyoncé's and (2) small-c creativity, which refers to being resolute and performing smaller acts of practical creativity every day (Beghetto and Kaufman, 2007). Small c creativity is the type that will thrive in a wellbeing committee, as it comes up with innovative and useful ideas on how to improve school community's wellbeing.

One way in which we can tap into our creative side is by brainstorming new ideas. Some of the mistakes often made when we brainstorm include judging the idea before we suggest it, which limits our creativity and makes the process negative. Being in a positive mood is essential as positive emotions open up our mind making us flexible problem-solvers (Isen, 2001). This is why before we embark on a brainstorming session, we need to create a positive environment for all committee members and allow them to generate wide-ranging and far-reaching options (Rawlinson, 1986).

There are various techniques for brainstorming, which include verbal/traditional brainstorming, nominal brainstorming and electronic brainstorming, which is sharing ideas via email or other digital devices (Al-Samarraie and Hurmuzan, 2018). In order to be effective, aimless idea-brainstorming should be avoided (Demir, 2005). Instead specific ideas addressing pertinent issues should be addressed. Brainstorming groups using verbal, traditional techniques are usually less effective in producing good ideas (Putman and Paulus, 2009) than people brainstorming on their own. This is why it is encouraged to use nominal brainstorming first, whereby individuals come up with new ideas on their own, and then do one of the three things: (1) bring their own ideas to a meeting and discuss; (2) share their ideas by email with the rest of the committee and discuss them during the next meeting; (3) share their ideas by email with one committee member, who then collates all ideas, enters them into document and analyses them for patterns, frequencies, originality or other criteria. This process will generate more creative ideas than engaging in a traditional brainstorming session. Let me give you an example.

Once the ideas are created, it is useful to engage in a democratic process of idea-prioritisation. All ideas are entered on flipchart sheets that are hanging on a wall. Each flipchart sheet may relate to a different community group, for example, ideas for parents, teachers, leaders, students; then each idea is explained, so that everyone has a clear understanding of its meaning. We give all committee members a marker each and ask them to put a star next to their top three ideas on each flipchart. They all walk around the room, putting stars next to the ideas they like. This generates the top ideas that the group has selected, which may be implemented as part of the school community wellbeing strategy and the wellbeing framework.

Framework

According to a review of many wellbeing programmes in schools, one of the important criteria for a programmes success is a framework used to guide the school's actions (Hung et al., 2014). A wellbeing framework is a theoretical model that underpins our actions and results in the school community's wellbeing improvement. The wellbeing framework used by schools can be either adapted from other frameworks or created specifically for a school. The existing frameworks applied in schools may come from research on wellbeing. Chapter 2 detailed a number of frameworks that derived from mixing various components of wellbeing, such as PERMA (Seligman, 2011) and its various alterations, such as PERMA-H, where H stands for physical health (Lai et al., 2018); PERMA-V, where V stands for vitality (Larby, 2017). Alternatively, other models may be applied, such as the national government's proposed model of wellbeing or international organisation's models, such as WHO, UNICEF and others.

Step 5: Share

Ideally, most of the work between step 1 and step 4 is completed by the end of the school year, so that the new year begins with the step 5. This step is about sharing information between the wellbeing committee and the school community and vice versa. It is recommended that as soon as the school year begins, the entire community is gathered together and the long-term vision (dream) for wellbeing in school is announced, along with the plans of activities for the coming year. Throughout the year, a two-way sharing process continues, whereby feedback from the initiatives is gathered regularly and shared with the school community. Also, an assessment of wellbeing is carried out at the beginning and at the end of the year to identify any changes in students' wellbeing. This information is shared with all during the last gathering of the year.

Creating a school's wellbeing strategy is one of the most hopeful things any school can do for their students. With a growing number of mental health issues among young people, it demonstrates that the school has not given up on its students. Its commitment to improving their health continues with determination, passion, kindness and care. Most importantly, however, the school's message is that creating a comprehensive, evidence-based wellbeing strategy for school is not a destination for achieving a point of optimal wellbeing, rather it is the beginning of a long journey, which the school chooses to take to improve the wellbeing of its entire community. For more ideas about implementing wellbeing in schools, please visit www.jolantaburke.com.

References

Al-Samarraie, H. & Hurmuzan, S. 2018. A review of brainstorming techniques in higher education. *Thinking Skills and Creativity*, 27, 78–91.

Bandura, A. & Albert, B. 1978. Self-efficacy: toward a unifying theory of behavioral change. *Advances in Behaviour Research and Therapy*, 1(4) 131–169.

Bas, S. & Tabancali, E. 2020. Correlations between teachers' personality, psychological safety perception and teacher voice. *Eurasian Journal of Educational Research*, 20, 185–204.

Beghetto, R. A. & Kaufman, J. C. 2007. Toward a broader conception of creativity: A case for 'mini-c' creativity. *Psychology of Aesthetics, Creativity, and the Arts*, 1, 73–79.

Brown, A. L. 1992. Design experiments: Theoretical and methodological challenges in creating complex interventions in classroom settings. *Journal of the Learning Sciences*, 2, 141.

Cooperrider, D. L. & McQuaid, M. 2012. *The Positive Arc of Systemic Strengths*, 46, 71–102.

Demir, Ç. 2005. Enhancing creativity in art education through brainstorming. *International Journal of Education through Art*, 1, 153–160.

Edmondson, A. 1999. Psychological safety and learning behavior in work teams. *Administrative Science Quarterly*, 44, 350–383.

Fredrickson, B. L. & Losada, M. F. 2005. Positive affect and the complex dynamics of human flourishing. *American Psychologist*, 60, 678–686.

Hung, T. T. M., Chiang, V. C. L., Dawson, A. & Lee, R. L. T. 2014. Understanding of factors that enable health promoters in implementing health-promoting schools: A systematic review and narrative synthesis of qualitative evidence. *PLoS ONE*, 9, 1–13.

Isen, A. M. 2001. An influence of positive affect on decision making in complex situations: Theoretical issues with practical implications. *Journal of Consumer Psychology*, 11, 75–85.

King, L. A. 2001. The health benefits of writing about life goals. *Personality and Social Psychology Bulletin*, 27, 798–807.

Lai, M. K., Leung, C., Kwok, S. Y. C., Hui, A. N. N., Lo, H. H. M., Leung, J. T. Y. & Tam, C. H. L. 2018. A multidimensional PERMA-H positive education model, general satisfaction of school life, and character strengths use in Hong Kong senior primary school students: Confirmatory factor analysis and path analysis using the APASO-II. *Frontiers in Psychology*, 9, 1090.

Larby, K. 2017. *What is wellbeing?* [Online]. Available: https://www.stac.school.nz/why-stac/well-being-at-stac/well-being-blog/what-is-well-being/ [Accessed 23rd Sep 2020].

Leiva, L., Zavala-Villalón, G., Antivilo-Bruna, A., Torres, B. & Ganga-León, C. 2020. Implementation of a national mental health intervention in educational communities: What do successful teams do differently? *Journal of Community Psychology*, 29, 2, 447–475.

Putman, V. L. & Paulus, P. B. 2009. Brainstorming, brainstorming rules and decision making. *The Journal of Creative Behavior*, 43, 23–39.

Rawlinson, J. G. 1986. *Creative Thinking and Brainstorming*. Aldershot: Gower.

Seligman, M. E. P. 2011. *Flourish: A Visionary New Understanding of Happiness and Well-Being*. New York: Atria.

Shalley, C. E., Zhou, J. & Oldham, G. R. 2010. The effects of personal and contextual characteristics on creativity: Where should we go from here? In: Wagner, J. A., III & Hollenbeck, J. R. (eds.), *Readings in Organizational Behavior*. New York: Routledge/Taylor & Francis Group.

Author index

Algoe Sarah 4, 34
Allen, Kelly-Ann 47, 89

Beghetto, Ronald A. 105
Belsky, Jay 78
Biswas-Diener, Robert 24
Boniwell, Ilona 20, 42, 44, 60, 78, 86, 87
Brown, Nick 80
Burke, Jolanta 1, 3, 5, 11, 18, 45, 46, 48, 62, 82
Burton, Chad M. 33

Csikszentmihalyi, Mihalyi 6, 19, 22, 42, 43

Davidson, Richard J. 23, 58
Deci, Edward 46, 80, 83
Diener, Ed 19–22, 24, 78, 89
Duckworth, Angela 51

Ekman, Paul 31
Emmons, Robert A. 4, 34

Fredrickson, Barbara 2, 4, 23, 29, 32, 33, 40, 49, 58, 80, 104
Froh, Jeffrey 34, 35

Gable, Shelley, 4, 34, 48
Glasser, William 48

Harzer, Claudia 46
Huppert, Felicia 21, 23

Isen, Alice 32, 106

Jung, Carl 20

Kahneman, Daniel 32, 46
Kaufman, James C. 105
Keyes, Corey 18, 21, 46
King, Laura A. 33, 37, 41, 49, 105

Layous, Kristin 34, 88–90
Linley, Alex 45
Lopez, Shane J. 40
Lyubomirsky, Sonja 3, 4, 24, 36, 39, 40, 49, 81, 84, 85, 88–90

Maslow, Abraham 8, 20
Mauss, Iris 79
McCullough, Michael E. 4, 34, 37
McGonigal, Kelly 61, 62
McGrath, Helen 22, 31, 40, 57, 97
McGrath, Robert 45

Neff, Kristin 38, 39
Niemiec, Ryan 45
Noble, Toni 22, 31, 40, 57
Norem, Julie 80
Parks, Acacia, 24
Pennebaker, James 38
Peterson, Christopher 19, 36, 44–46, 56
Pluess, Michael 77, 78, 97

Quinlan, Denise 45

Reivich, Karen 37, 97, 99
Rogers, Carl 20, 56
Rotter, Julian 54
Ruch, Willibald 46, 58
Ryan, Richard M. 46, 80, 83
Ryff, Carol 19–21, 49

Schwartz, Barry 84, 85
Segerstrom, Suzanne 80
Seligman, Martin 6, 12, 19–22, 34, 35, 44, 45, 50, 51, 54–57, 78, 82, 90, 106

Snyder, Charles R. 40, 42
Steger, Michael F. 49, 50

Vailliant, George E. 12, 20, 46
Vallerand, Robert J. 51

Waters, Lea 34, 89
Wong, Paul T.P. 49, 50
Wood, Alex M. 4, 34
Worthington, Everett 35, 36

Subject index

ABCDE disputation 57
acceptance 20; mindful acceptance 86; self-acceptance 20, 21; social acceptance 21
accomplishment 20, 21, 50–53; *see also* achievement
achievement 25, 31, 51, 54
ACTIONS model 86
active-constructive responding 48, 86
acts of kindness 2, 24, 48, 49, 84, 85, 88
alcohol misuse 1, 60
anger 30, 31, 35–37, 55, 81, 85, 97
anxiety 11, 18, 23, 24, 30–32, 36, 38, 56, 60, 62, 79, 84, 89, 97, 99
appreciation 34, 85, 102, 104–105
authentic pride *see* pride
autonomy 5, 19, 21, 53–55
avoiding overthinking 48, 85
awe 33

benefit finding 37
bereavement 37, 38, 57
best possible school 41
best possible self 41, 84–87, 105
BINGO cards 48
boredom 34, 41, 42
Bounce Back! Programme 57, 97
Broaden-and-build theory 32
Building Hope for the Future programme 40
bullying 18, 36, 45, 57, 78, 83, 97, 99
burnout 31

career wellbeing 12, 20
CARES model 102–107
Changing your critical self-talk 39
character strengths *see* strengths
choices 35, 41, 44, 50, 55, 56, 83–87, 97
cognitive behavioural therapy (CBT) 32
committing to your goals 84, 85
community wellbeing xi, 20, 106
compassion 32, 35, 36, 38–39, 86, 89
compassion break 39
conflict 30, 36, 57
control 33, 40, 42, 43, 51–55, 57, 62, 80, 81, 83
COVID-19 1, 10, 16
creativity 34, 105–106
Cultivating Awareness and Resilience in Education 11
cultivating optimism 84, 85, 86
cultural fit 96, 98

daily hassles 57–58
dancing 53, 59, 86
decisional forgiveness 35–36
defensive pessimism 80
depression 4, 9–11, 18, 23, 24, 30–32, 34, 35, 38, 39, 50, 52, 54, 56, 60, 62, 78, 79, 84, 88–90, 97, 99
developing strategies for coping 40, 84, 85
dignity 8, 9, 11, 57, 86
disability 97

disorder 1, 18, 23, 24, 30, 38, 60, 87
dispositional optimism *see* optimism
distributed leadership 55
diversity 9, 98
doing more activities that truly engage you 84, 85
Dual Continua Model *see* Mental Health Continuum

emotional forgiveness 35–37; *see also* forgiveness
emotional intelligence 30—31
engagement 8, 20–22, 34, 41–45, 47, 55, 59, 60, 86, 88, 97
ENTRÉE programme 97
environmental mastery 19, 21
epigenetics 77–78
EPOCH 22, 23
eudaemonic wellbeing 5, 19, 20
explanatory styles *see* optimism
expressing gratitude 3, 34, 84, 85
expressive writing 38, 87

financial wellbeing 20
flourishing 18, 19, 22, 23, 26, 32, 49
FLOURISH model 22
flow 42–44, 53, 60
forgiveness 35–37, 86, 87
forgiveness letter 35, 36, 87
Friends for Life Programme 97, 99
funeral service/epitaph 87

Gallup 20, 62, 63
Gift of time 49
gratitude 3, 10, 12, 33–35, 45, 48, 84–86, 89; journal 48, 85; visit 86
GRIT 51

harmonious passion *see* passion
healthy eating 18, 23, 25, 60
hedonic wellbeing 5, 19, 20
hope 5, 23, 32–35, 39–41, 86, 107
How would you treat a friend ? 39
hubristic pride *see* pride
humour 33, 45, 58

implementation intention 41
insomnia 34, 97
intensely positive experience 33
International Positive Education Network (IPEN) 96

interventions: ABCDE disputation 57; active-constructive responding 48, 86; acts of kindness 2, 24, 48, 49, 84, 85, 88; avoiding overthinking 48, 85; benefit finding 37; best possible school 41; best possible self- 41, 84–87, 105; BINGO cards 48; *Changing your critical self-talk* 39; committing to your goals 84, 85; compassion break 39; cultivating optimism 84, 85, 86; developing strategies for coping 40, 84, 85; doing more activities that truly engage you 84, 85; expressing gratitude 3, 34, 84, 85; expressive writing 38, 87; forgiveness letter 35, 36, 87; funeral service/epitaph 87; *Gift of Time* 49; gratitude journal 48, 85; gratitude visit 86; *How would you treat a friend ?* 39; implementation intention 41; intensely positive experience 33; involvement in community projects 87; learning to forgive 36–37, 84–86; Lego Serious Play 82; letter of forgiveness *see* forgiveness letter; letting go of grudges 37; mindfulness meditation 50, 86; most Feared obituary 50, 86; nurturing relationships 84, 85; *One door closes another door opens* 58, 86; playlist 87; positive affirmations 4; positive portfolio 87; positive reminiscence 86, 87; practicing religion or spirituality 45, 85; REACH model 36; savouring life's joys 52–53, 84–87; sky-gazing 7, 24; taking care of your body 84, 85; three funny things 86; three good things 34, 48, 86; *What went well* 35, 87; wise feedback intervention 44; worry reduction 87
involvement in community projects 87
IPEN 96
isolation 47

Kids Supporting Kids 37
kindness 8, 12, 24, 35, 36, 38, 39, 44, 48, 49, 84–86, 88

languishing 18, 26
learning to forgive 36–37, 84–86
Lego Serious Play 82
letter of forgiveness *see* forgiveness letter

letting go of grudges 37
life purpose 5, 19, 21, 32, 49–50
life satisfaction 19, 21, 24, 34, 40, 45
locus of control 54–55
love 10, 32, 33, 45, 48, 61
loving kindness meditation 2, 86

meaningful life 19, 46
mental contrasting 41
Mental Health Continuum 18–19, 21
mindfulness 11, 38, 50, 83, 84, 86–88, 97
mindfulness meditation 50, 86
Mindfulness-based Stress Reduction 11, 97
Mindfulness-based Stress Reduction Programme 11, 97
MindMatters 98
mood 10, 11, 31, 33, 35, 38, 49, 60, 106
MoodGym 97
Most Feared Obituary 50, 86
motivation 41–43, 60, 61, 80, 83, 84, 86, 90, 104

negative emotions 19, 21, 31–33, 37–39, 51, 58, 78, 81, 97
New Beginning Parent Programme 98
nurture room 29
nurturing relationships 84, 85

Ob Volle Kracht 98
obsessive passion *see* passion
One door closes another door opens 58, 86
optimism 21–23, 34, 40, 55–57, 58, 80, 84–87, 97

passion 51–52, 107
pedagogy 12–13, 42
Penn Resiliency Programme 97, 98
PERMA model 20–22, 51, 82, 106
personal growth 21
personality 42, 46
personally valued goals 49
philosophical paradigms 5, 19
physical activity 42, 53, 54, 59–60, 85, 86, 90
physical exercise 59, 86
physical wellbeing 8, 20
playlist 87
positive affirmations 4
positive education 20, 98
positive emotions 19, 21, 23, 24, 31–35, 38, 42, 49–51, 55, 78–81, 89, 106

positive illusion *see* optimism
positive portfolio 87
positive psychology interventions 24; *see also* interventions
positive reminiscence 86, 87
practicing religion or spirituality 45, 85
present-oriented 77, 87
pride 30, 33, 51–52
programmes: *Bounce Back!* Programme 57, 97; *Cultivating Awareness and Resilience in Education* 11; *Kids Supporting Kids* 37; *Mindfulness-based Stress Reduction Programme* 11, 97; *MindMatters* 98; *MoodGym* 97; *New Beginning Parent* Programme 98; Ob Volle Kracht 98; *Penn Resiliency* Programme 97, 98; PRP *see Penn Resiliency* Programme ; *Rock and Water* Programme 96; *Safe Routes to School* Programme 60; *7 Humour Habits* programme 58; ENTRÉE programme 97; *Friends for Life* Programme 97, 99; *SPARK* Programme 97; *Zippy Friends* 2, 99
PROSPER model 22
PRP *see Penn Resiliency* Programme
psychological wellbeing 5, 12, 19, 21, 58, 59, 79
PURE model 50

Quality of Life therapy 50

REACH model 36
Relationships 4, 5, 11, 20–22, 34, 39, 43, 46–48, 57, 60, 84–86, 89, 95
Resilience 11, 20–22, 32, 52, 57–58, 86, 89, 97
Rock and Water Programme 96
Rumination 34

Safe Routes to School Programme 60
savouring life's joys 52–53, 84–87
school-belonging 7, 46–48
school climate 8–9, 36
self-acceptance 19, 21, 22
self-awareness 5, 11, 52
self-compassion *see* compassion
self-control *see* control
self-esteem 4, 21, 23, 24, 42, 45, 52
self-regulation 87
self-selection 84–86
7 Humour Habits programme 58

shame 8, 35, 38, 51
sky-gazing 7, 24
social support 32, 57, 88
social wellbeing 4, 20, 21
SPARK Programme 97
strengths 5, 12, 22, 25, 44–46, 50, 60, 86, 87, 89, 103–105
stress 2, 4, 5, 10, 11, 19, 23, 26, 31, 33, 34, 36, 37, 39, 49, 50, 54, 58, 61–63, 80, 85, 87, 97
stress mindset 62–63
subjective wellbeing 5, 19, 20, 21
substance abuse 60

taking care of your body 84, 85
third culture kids (TCK) 47
three funny things 86
three good things 34, 48, 86

UN 1
UNESCO 1, 17
unhappy 11, 12, 50, 54, 79, 91, 93
UNICEF 1, 20, 82, 106

values 8, 9, 12, 36, 40, 44, 47, 48, 105
values-in-action *see* strengths

wellbeing interventions *see* interventions
wellbeing programmes *see* programmes
What went well 35, 87
WHO 1, 4, 5, 20, 24, 59, 60, 82, 99
wise feedback intervention 44
wishful thinking *see* optimism
World Health Organisation *see* WHO
worry reduction 87

Zippy Friends 2, 99

For Product Safety Concerns and Information please contact our EU
representative GPSR@taylorandfrancis.com
Taylor & Francis Verlag GmbH, Kaufingerstraße 24, 80331 München, Germany

www.ingramcontent.com/pod-product-compliance
Lightning Source LLC
Chambersburg PA
CBHW082102230426
43670CB00017B/2925